A New Day In Christ

How to Calm Stress and Anxiety in Twenty Minutes a Day

JIM OTREMBA, M.DIV, M.S., LICSW

A New Day In Christ: How to Calm Stress and Anxiety in Twenty Minutes a Day
Copyright © 2016 Jim Otremba, M.Div., M.S., LICSW.

All rights reserved. No part of this workbook may be reproduced, transmitted, or stored in any form whatsoever, printed or electronic, without the prior written permission of the author.

Stress Snapshot Questionnaire. Copyright© 2009 Jim Otremba, M.Div., M.S., LICSW.

Scripture quoted from the *Holy Bible, New Century Version®*, Copyright © 1987, 1988, 1991, by Word Publishing, a division of Thomas Nelson, Inc. Used by permission. All rights reserved.

This workbook is not intended to diagnose or treat any mental or physical disorder. Nor is it meant to replace any professional treatment for any disorder. If you have severe symptoms of anxiety, stress, or other major disorders please seek professional help. The author assumes no responsibility for misuse of this material.

Printed and Manufactured in the United States of America
1 2 3 4 5 6 7 8 9 10

Contents

Foreword 4
Preface/How to Use This Workbook 5
Stress Snapshot Questionnaire 8
Strategy 1: Name and Tame Your "Time-i-cides" 11
Strategy 2: Name and Reframe the Sources of Stress 15
Strategy 3: Breath is Holy 17
Strategy 4: The Peaceful Reality of Association 21
Strategy 5: You are Not the Problem 23
Strategy 6: Forgiveness Fundamentals 25
Strategy 7: Identify and Work Through Grief Issues via Romans 8:28 29
Strategy 8: The Power of Water and Oil 31
Strategy 9: Understand the Pros and Cons of Your Images of God 33
Strategy 10: The School of Stress 35
Strategy 11: Navigate Wisely Those People Whose Actions Increase Your Stress 37
Strategy 12: Enter into Daily Sabbath Moments 39
Strategy 13: Christian Meditation 43
Strategy 14: Name and Tame "Emotional Illusions" 47
Strategy 15: Identity is More Important than Personality 49
Strategy 16: Listen to the Word, not to the Wounds 51
Strategy 17: Understand and Use Your Imagination 53
Strategy 18: Examine the Difference Between Shame and Guilt 57
Strategy 19: The Muscle of Music 59
Strategy 20: Lessons from Your Family of Origin and Your Origin of Family 61
Strategy 21: The New is in the Now 65
Strategy 22: Got Anger? Get a Plan 69
Strategy 23: GIGO Applies to Stress and Anxiety 73
Strategy 24: Use Productive and Proactive Recreational Time 79
Strategy 25: Name and Re-Write Your Negative "MP3 Files" 81
Closing Thoughts 84
Cut-Out Reminders 85, 87, 90
Scriptural Reminders About Who I Am 89
Follow-Up Chart 92
Post-Stress Snapshot Questionnaire 94
About the Author 97
What Others Have Said About the Otrembas' Material 98

Foreword

In my psychiatric practice, I have seen Christians who have experienced the horrible, unrelenting effects of anxiety. Uncontrolled anxiety can fill you with worry, zap your energy, kill your spirit, and steal your joy. You may be caught in a spiral of frustration and defeat.

Treating anxiety requires an approach that may include anti-anxiety medications and psychotherapy or Christian counseling. But medication, while often life saving, and counseling, which is essential to recovery, often doesn't completely eradicate the symptoms of anxiety or restore peace. Recovery needs to include a daily game plan to ease anxiety. This is why I am so enthused about this workbook.

In these pages, Jim has provided practical, Scripturally based, psychologically sound tools to effectively manage stress and anxiety. I like these techniques and exercises because they lower immediate levels of stress and tension. And most importantly, with daily practice, chronic anxiety symptoms can gradually become much less intense and easier to manage.

I have had the privilege of working with patients who have used these principles and techniques; the results have been impressive. My prayer is that you, too, will find daily encouragement, help, and reassurance as you begin to use this workbook.

—*Dean Watkins, M.D.*

Preface: Stress is Inevitable; Anxiety is Optional

The Psalmist says, "I am fearfully and wonderfully made!" Indeed, we are. The Lord has blessed His crown of creation, the human race, with an incredible mind, body, and soul.

Before I briefly describe how stress is inevitable, but anxiety is optional, it's good to recognize that it's far beyond the scope of this workbook to go into depth on these systems. Still, it's helpful to have a basic understanding of these miracles that we sometimes take for granted.

Before the fall of humanity described in Genesis 3, it's reasonable to believe that we had no stress or anxiety. But after the fall we can't escape the reality of stress. Even the beginning of our life is stressful.

When the egg and sperm meet and create a new person, the resulting individual immediately and automatically creates a hard "shell" so no more sperm can enter in: this is the stressful reality of protection. Stress happens at a cellular level when our cells divide for the first time and slowly begin to create new organs and systems. These are examples of "good" stress: stress that's needed for us to grow and be protected. There's also toxic stress that happens at a biological level when a virus or bacteria invade, trying to wreak havoc. Because stress is everywhere, God has given us an intricate system to help us maintain our balance in stressful times.

This system that God gives us helps us to excel or know when we're in trouble. It's a division of the autonomic nervous system called the sympathetic nervous system (SNS). The SNS is a vast network that helps us move, think, feel, and even perform to the highest of our abilities (the "peak-performance" of the SNS). When athletes are "in the zone," the "zone" is the silent miracle we call the SNS.

But, like all things God created, there's a sacred order implicit in this division of the autonomic nervous system. And like most difficulties, problems start developing when we are out of balance and the sacred order that God intended breaks down. This lack of balance happens when the SNS goes beyond its peak performance and no longer is in regulation with the "counter-part" of the SNS. The "counter-part" of the SNS is called the para-sympathetic nervous system (PSNS). The PSNS is critically important for balance; it's the "rest and digest" part of the nervous system.

Here's an easy way to remember the difference between these two miracles: the sympathetic nervous system (SNS) starts with an "S." The word "stress" starts with an "S" as well. The words "para-sympathetic nervous system" (PSNS) start with a "P." And the word "peace" starts with a "P." It's no coincidence that the Lord leaves His peace to us during the Last Supper in the Gospel of John. Jesus tells his apostles, and us, "Peace I leave you, my peace I give to you" (John 14:27). Jesus—the great healer—tells us that He wants us to be in total balance, in right relationship, with Abba, Himself, the Spirit, and others. This right relationship is maintained by the para-sympathetic nervous system.

When we're fresh from God at birth, we naturally understand this! Unless an infant is born to a mother using too many drugs, or the baby has medical conditions, a newborn understands in her body how to stay para-sympathetically dominant—teaching us adults profound lessons. Consider that when you were a newborn, you came into this world with the innate ability to breathe deeply. These deep diaphragm breaths helped keep you para-sympathetically dominant! This is just one of the many profound lessons that newborns teach us.

This ability to breathe deeply helps the newborn stay balanced. But then life happens. Stress happens, and we forget how to stay balanced and get stressed out. Our parents might yell at us (raising our stress hormones and triggering our sympathetic nervous system), or we grow up thinking we have no control over anxiety. We forget the lesson we knew in our bodies as infants, and we no longer breathe from the diaphragm. This lack of deep breathing, as well as other essentials intended to help us stay calm, can lead to us being sympathetically dominant, which increases our stress.

When we stay in the sympathetic nervous system too long, it can lead to anxiety. That's the reason I say stress is inevitable but anxiety is optional. For those who wrestle with anxiety, it doesn't feel optional. But the truth is, for those of us who were not born with major difficulties, we innately know how to stay balanced as a newborn. This para-sympathetic dominance is then lost as we slowly get out of the practice of balance. The more balance we have, the more para-sympathetically dominant we are, just as we were when we were born. Stress will continue in our lives, and some of it will be toxic, but as long as we practice ways to stay in balance, that stress doesn't have to lead to anxiety.

One of the keys to making sure our stress doesn't lead to anxiety is to create daily habits that will keep us para-sympathetically dominant. The rest of this workbook is full of ideas on how to do just that.

Prayer

God of peace, thank you that your only Son prayed that I be at peace in my life. This prayer of Christ is all-powerful! Send me your Holy Spirit so that I may now open up my mind, body, and soul to the para-sympathetic dominance that Christ desires. Bless me as I journey into this peace through using the suggestions in this workbook. May it lead me to true peace. Amen.

How to Use This Workbook

Before you start, I invite you to take my "Stress Snapshot Questionnaire." There's another copy of this questionnaire at the end of this workbook so you can compare your progress after using this workbook for the recommended 30-60 days.

My hope is that you'll use this workbook for about 20 minutes each day for the next 30-60 days. The workbook offers 25 strategies that have helped many of my clients calm anxiety and create a healthier response to stress. Because each of us has different levels of stress and anxiety, I've tried to include the top strategies that continue to help the many people the Lord brings to our office each week. While you're practicing the recommendations, keep track of the top seven or so (crease the top of the page or write down the page number so you can easily find it). These can become your "go-to" responses when stress is high. This will allow you the opportunity to acquire new and healthier responses to stress or anxiety and these new responses can become habits for the rest of your stress-reduced life!

You'll also notice at the end of the workbook a section called "Cut-Out Reminders." This section has reminders that you can cut out; post them where you can see them and use them to lower your stress. You'll also find follow-up charts that will help you track your peaceful response. Some pages are intentionally blank; feel free to use them to write notes.

I include multiple strategies because you may already be using some of them. If you're using one of them, simply skip over that one and you'll still find new suggestions to calm anxiety and lower stress in just 20 minutes a day. If you find that a recommendation is working well, stick with that for a few days before you add a new one. This format allows for some individualization to create your own personal stress reduction program. I want this to be a dynamic, interactive experience the Lord can use, and not a stiff pre-set list of rules.

May the Holy Spirit bless you right now with peace. And may Christ, who remembers and redeems stress, bless you with healing and abundant life. Amen.

Stress Snapshot Questionnaire

Date_____

Directions:

Start by dating this questionnaire. This will serve as a reminder of how your stress levels can change in just 20 minutes a day while you go through and implement the ideas in this workbook. If you feel so inclined, share your answers with your spouse or loved one for objective feedback to your answers. You'll find a copy of this questionnaire at the end of the workbook, so you can see how the Holy Spirit is bringing peace into your life in 20 minutes a day.

Circle the appropriate number for each item.
0 = Never 1 = Not Often 2 = Occasionally 3 = Frequently 4 = Mostly 5 = Always

When you're done, add up your total. There are three categories to this inventory: Body, Mind, and Soul/Relationships. I use three categories because stress and anxiety can alter different aspects of our lives. If you have severe symptoms of anxiety, please see your doctor as soon as possible.

Body

	Never	Not Oft.	Occasion.	Frequent.	Mostly	Always
1. Jaw tightness/clenching teeth	0	1	2	3	4	5
2. Heart racing	0	1	2	3	4	5
3. Stomach upset or "gurgling"	0	1	2	3	4	5
4. Headaches or migraines	0	1	2	3	4	5
5. Nervous habits (nail biting, etc.)	0	1	2	3	4	5
6. Muscle tightness	0	1	2	3	4	5
7. Back pain	0	1	2	3	4	5
8. Furrowed brow	0	1	2	3	4	5
9. Dizziness and/or chest pain	0	1	2	3	4	5
10. Unhealthy or emotional eating	0	1	2	3	4	5
11. Alcohol or drug misuse	0	1	2	3	4	5

Total from Body category = _____

(if there are serious Body stressors, please see your doctor immediately).

Mind

	Never	Not Oft.	Occasion.	Frequent.	Mostly	Always
12. Worry about things I can't change	0	1	2	3	4	5
13. Daily negative self-statements	0	1	2	3	4	5
14. Making mountains out of molehills	0	1	2	3	4	5
15. More pessimistic, less optimistic	0	1	2	3	4	5
16. Not sleeping well	0	1	2	3	4	5
17. Watching the nightly news	0	1	2	3	4	5
18. Feeling irrational fears	0	1	2	3	4	5
19. "Hamster on the wheel" thoughts	0	1	2	3	4	5
20. Perfectionist or "type A"	0	1	2	3	4	5
21. Reading negative articles or news	0	1	2	3	4	5
22. Watching secular movies	0	1	2	3	4	5
23. Watching secular TV	0	1	2	3	4	5

Total from Mind category = _____

Soul/Relationships

	Never	Not Oft.	Occasion.	Frequent.	Mostly	Always
24. Not being patient with self or others	0	1	2	3	4	5
25. Using harsh words	0	1	2	3	4	5
26. Using sarcasm or unhealthy tones	0	1	2	3	4	5
27. Not forgiving of others	0	1	2	3	4	5
28. Not forgiving of self	0	1	2	3	4	5
29. No regular public worship	0	1	2	3	4	5
30. Hopeless or helpless feelings	0	1	2	3	4	5
31. Lack of daily gratitude	0	1	2	3	4	5
32. Not much emotional or verbal closeness with others	0	1	2	3	4	5
33. Not many close friends I trust	0	1	2	3	4	5
34. My relationships feel hurtful	0	1	2	3	4	5
35. I don't feel respected by those who are supposed to love me	0	1	2	3	4	5
36. Negative image of God (God is only a judge and is harsh on you)	0	1	2	3	4	5

Total from Soul/Relationships category.............._____
Total from Body category (from page 8).............._____
Total from Mind category (from page 9)............_____

Grand Total.._____

Key

0 – 15...........Negligible Stress
31 – 45..........Mild Stress
56 – 80..........High Stress
81 – 180.......Severe Stress (*professional help is recommended*)

16 – 30.........Low Stress
46 – 55.........Moderate Stress

Notice: This questionnaire is not intended to be used for professional diagnostic purposes, nor is it a psychological inventory. The author assumes no liability for misuse of this questionnaire.
© 2009, James C. Otremba, M.Div., M.S., LICSW.

Strategy 1: Name and Tame Your "Time-i-cides"

"There is a time for everything, and everything on earth has its special season." —Ecclesiastes 3:1

"Time-i-cides" are everywhere in our society. Some of us, myself included, have been taught to develop habits that literally kill time. This is not helpful when it comes to calming anxiety and managing stress.

On the other hand, there are those of us who don't kill any time; our calendars are jam-packed and we're still very stressed out and anxious. If you're in this category I invite you to put this workbook down and grab your calendar or electronic scheduler. Then, if you want to, schedule 20 minutes per day to read this workbook. Schedule that for the next 30 days so you can develop new habits to lower your response to stress. If you have no "time-i-cides," feel free to skip the next few pages (unless you're curious about those of us who kill time—a foreign concept to you) and go right to Strategy 2 on page 15 for more information on practical ways to calm anxiety and lower stress.

As a Gen-X-er, I was raised with the beginning of video games (remember the old ping-pong TV games?), infant computers (nothing like we have now), and nearly unlimited TV time. I thought this was my "downtime" and time to "relax." I was almost taught that wasting time (in my case, killing time in front of a screen) is a good thing. After I graduated from college and finished my first graduate degree in Theology, I earned another graduate degree in Applied Psychology. It was during this second graduate degree program that I began to study brain physiology and how time in front of screens is not downtime, nor is it relaxing.

God made the brain one big chemical and electrical factory . . . it's truly amazing! Psalm 139:14 states it best, ". . . you made me in an amazing and wonderful way." There are about 100 billion cells called neurons that compose this masterpiece, and they never touch each other. They communicate with each other via a complex web of electrical impulses and neurotransmitters (chemicals). The brain also offers us a paradox that we would do well to apply to our hectic, stress-filled, lives: it's most at rest when it's active with a purpose. Not busy with just "stuff" to do, or a "busy body" as St. Paul would call it, but assertively active or active with a calming purpose (for example, Christian meditation). Let me explain.

It's during Rapid Eye Movement sleep (REM) that the brain is very active. The brain is so active—with a purpose of healing and restoring—during REM sleep that the body is literally paralyzed so it can't act on the REM dreams. It's also during the deep sleep stages that the brain actually regenerates and rejuvenates itself in a most mysterious manner. The brain is most restful and re-creational when it's most active.

If we could apply this bio-chemical truth to our stress management, it would transform the way we view downtime. Yes, we need downtime and recreational time. But not in the form of watching most of what is on TV, or surfing most websites, because the majority of these activities are passive and unproductive activities at best. I call these "unproductive screentime." At its worst, this screentime can be death dealing and a trap to allure us into "soft porn" (I hate that phrase because lust is lust), gambling, spending too much money, or just about any other enslavement that excessive and unproductive screentime can bring. Not all screentime is created equal, so we need to pray about the type of things we're watching and make sure they're truly recreational and honor God. Here's a good discernment question: could I watch what I'm watching right now with Jesus next to me? This question may help us discern unproductive screentime versus more productive screentime.

If screentime isn't recreational, then what is? This workbook is full of ideas. We need silence, meditation, appreciating beauty, art, music, prayer, conversation (especially with our loved ones), nature, journaling, exercising, gardening, sewing, martial arts (one of my favorites), creating scrapbooks (one of my wife's favorites), teaching, reading, writing (another favorite!), singing, and more. All of these activities are recreational and can eventually replace unproductive screentime and lower stress.

When I learned about the biology of the brain and the paradoxes it offers, it really opened up my eyes to see how mind-numbing TV and unproductive screentime can be. Fundamentally, this insight has changed most aspects of my life, including my anxiety levels and stress management. I was guilty of killing time via watching too much TV. That was my major time-i-cide. How about you? Are there any major ways you kill time? Please take five minutes and ask the Holy Spirit to help you identify any major time-killers you may have. Name them here:

Now that you've named them, let's start to tame them. If you're killing time, set aside a percentage of that time and re-invest it into reading and using this workbook every day so you can learn new ways to transform daily stress. For example, if you kill two hours a day, take 25 percent (30 minutes) and reinvest it into reading and using these strategies every day for 20 minutes each day.

Date:_____

1) My current major time-killers are:

2) Which of the above time-i-cides will you start to tame by reinvesting them into using these recommendations to lower your stress?

Prayer About Good Time Stewardship

All good and loving God, you give me the precious gift of time so that I can become transformed into your image and likeness. Send me your Spirit today so that I can use time wisely. Help me to start seeing the tremendous gift that time is and how it can be used to lower my stress. In the name of Christ our Lord, and in his Spirit, I pray. Amen.

Strategy 2: Name and Reframe the Sources of Your Stress

"Look at the birds in the air. They don't plant or harvest or store food in barns, but your heavenly Father feeds them." —Matthew 6:26

Now that you've identified some time-i-cides in your life (or you didn't need to and you're on this strategy), it's good to name and reframe the many sources of stress that you feel.

It's essential to know the sources of stress and which stress you can and can't control. By naming a stressful dynamic in our lives we begin to exert dominion over it. Christ has authority over everything (Mark 1:27, Eph. 1:22, I Cor. 15:28). The great news is that we share in the identity of Christ (Rom. 8:10). We are members of the Body of Christ, and Christ desires to dwell in us and share His authority with us (2 Cor. 13:10, Rev. 2:28) so we have authority over dynamics in our lives. We need to act on that reality and name the sources of stress in our lives. Start today. Take time to write out the major stressors in your life. This exercise can be enhanced by letting an ally (spouse, best friend, trusted co-worker) share with you some observations on what he or she believes your stressors are.

Date:_____

These are the major stressors in my life:

Now that you've named the sources of stress in your life, start to "re-frame" them by grouping them into three categories:

1) Stresses you can't control. 2) Stresses you partially control (marriage, work, etc.). 3) Stresses you can directly control (what you eat, if you watch TV, etc.).

For example, you may have the economy on your stress list on page 15. Consider how much direct control you have over the economy. Not much at all. Decide which others you do not control and cross them off your list. As you cross them off the list, give yourself verbal permission not to worry about them today. Something that usually accompanies this exercise is the realization that much of our stress is outside of our realm of control. This can be freeing to see on paper.

Use the past tense to let these go: tell yourself "In the past I used to worry about you, but now I see that I have no direct control over you and so I will not worry about you today." Tell the worries in this category: "I need to save my energy for the next two categories; I don't have time for you anymore." The more you tell yourself this message, the more you will slowly start believing it and thereby evict this entire category from your thoughts, one day at time. It's easier said than done, but if it isn't said it won't get done. We have to talk very positively to ourselves and recognize who we are as members of the Body of Christ and children of God. Christ desires that we have dominion over seeing what we truly can and can't control.

Now we need to develop a working plan for the second and third categories: worries you partially control and worries you directly control. The focus of this work is to understand that we have a loving God who gives us the power to develop new responses to stress and lower our anxiety.

How does it help to know that in Christ you have dominion over your stressful dynamics?

Prayer About Naming and Reframing Stress

All powerful God, you so lovingly share your power of naming dynamics with us through your son Jesus, who is Lord of all. At Jesus' name, every knee has to bend, including the knees of my worries and fears. Send your Spirit of strength so that I can claim dominion over stress in my life, and please give me wisdom to see what I can and can't control. Help me to practice these recommendations and thus bring peace into my life. Amen.

Strategy 3: Breath is Holy

"He breathed the breath of life into the man's nose, and the man became a living person." —Genesis 2:7

Being a part-time stay-at-home dad has been such a blessing. I remember sneaking into the bedroom when our children were infants and watching them sleep. So beautiful! Have you had that experience? If you're not a parent, have you watched an infant sleep? Do you remember what part of their body moves while they sleep? The answer to this question is critically important to stress management (you'll find it in the next paragraph). When we think about this answer we recognize that infants, fresh from God, have much to teach us about stress management.

Little infants, when they sleep, take wonderful deep breaths; their little tummies move. This is perfect form for a full diaphragmatic breath. The diaphragm is a parachute-shaped muscle that separates the heart and lungs from the stomach and other organs. A breath from the diaphragm means that the breath is going down to the lower portion of the lung, thereby causing the diaphragm to push the belly button out. This type of slow diaphragmatic breath is wonderful for stress because it can lower the heart rate, slow the body down, and eventually interrupt some hormone stress sequences in the body.

If you're not doing deep breathing, please start today. It's simple to start if you remember that you're not learning something new. When you were a newborn you did this automatically, as all infants do. But life gets in the way and we forget. Here's how you can remember:

It's easiest to correctly breathe from the diaphragm when you're on your back. Take a few minutes right now and practice the proper way to breathe. Lie down on your bed and place one hand on your chest and one on your belly button. Think about the Trinity (Father, Son, Holy Spirit): breathe in for three seconds, hold the breath for three seconds, and then exhale for three seconds. As you do this, the only hand that should move is the hand on your belly button. Don't hyperventilate, but relax and focus on your breath for a couple of minutes; think about how holy and essential breathing is. While you're doing your deep breathing, focus on breathing in the Holy Spirit's love for you and exhaling out the stress of the day; give it all to God. You can even start to breathe out the stressors—those you partially control and those you have direct control over from the previous chapter.

Humans can live for weeks without food and days without water, but only a few short minutes without breath. God breathed the breath of life into us (Gen. 2:7), and the Hebrew word for "spirit" in the Old Testament is "ruah," which can also be translated into "breath." Furthermore, how did Jesus decide to give the apostles the Holy Spirit? Yes, Jesus breathed on them (John 20:22) and sent His Spirit. When we breathe, we're praying. That's often missed in our rushed-along, hurry-up and finish society.

Deep breathing can also slow down our speech. Slowing down our speech patterns is also important in stress-management. Many of us talk quickly, and when we hear ourselves talk quickly, this can actually increase our stress and anxiety. Today's recommendation of deep breathing can help slow us down in many ways. I recall how this recommendation helped my client Bill.

Bill is a wonderful Christian and specialized medical doctor who experienced tremendous stress throughout his daily duties. Bill reported that he always felt rushed and impatient with others. He was frustrated with the pace of his life and didn't know what to do.

He had never done any intentional deep breathing, so I taught him what I'm teaching you right now. He tried it and liked it. He noticed that the stress he was experiencing seemed to lessen, based on deep breathing and slowing down. Of course he didn't get it perfect right away. These recommendations aren't about perfection, but about progress. He did make progress and after practicing a few more of these recommendations he wrote me a thank you note, telling me how his life felt less stressful. In addition, all of his professional and personal relationships benefited from his deep breathing and slowing down as well.

Deep breathing has helped countless people manage their daily stress. If you're not consistently practicing deep breathing and slowing down, please try it right now. You'll be amazed at how calming it can be. Again, when you do it, focus on breathing in God's tremendous love for you, and when you exhale, breathe out all the worries and stress that you have been feeling for the day, the week, the month, or the year. Let it all out. The Holy Spirit desires that we let go of our worries and cares (I Pet. 5:7).

Reflection Questions About Deep Breathing

1) When can you make time to do some deep breathing today?

2) How will it help to focus on breathing in the Spirit of God's love and exhaling the stress of the day, week, month, or year?

3) If you talk too quickly, how will it help to focus on slowing down your pace?

Prayer About Deep Breathing

All good and gentle God, you give me the power today to start deep breathing and slowing down. Send your Holy Spirit into my heart so that I can practice breathing in your love for me and breathing out the stress of the day. Slow down my talking and help me to realize anew your calming love for me. I pray this through Christ our Lord, and in the power of your Holy Spirit. Amen.

Strategy 4: The Peaceful Reality of Associations

"May the Lord watch over you and give you peace." —Numbers 6:26

Deep breathing is usually taught in most stress-management books because it works. But there's another technique that works in conjunction with deep breathing, and when they're paired together and practiced consistently and correctly, they work as a major stress killer.

Once you've practiced the correct way to deep breathe for a few days (without hyperventilating) and you can do it almost anywhere (at a meeting, in your car, sitting down, standing up, at a grocery check-out counter, etc.) start associating every stressful situation with prayer, an affirming word to yourself, and deep breathing. Yes, deep breathing is good, but associating stress with prayer, an affirming word, and deep breathing is excellent! It works so well because it calms mind, body, and soul all together. The prayer calms your soul, the self-affirming words calm your mind, and the deep breathing calms your body.

I remember working with Betty, a very insightful, committed Christian. She knew the sources of her stress, and she was practicing some of the major stress reduction techniques that I like to teach. She was deep breathing daily and was using some Christian meditation, another recommendation later in the workbook. But she didn't associate stress with prayer. When people try this technique they love it because it heals mind, body, and soul. Here's how to start:

Practice deep breathing every day until it becomes natural. Then, start to tell yourself "Today when I feel stress I will associate it with a short prayer, an affirming word to myself, and deep breathing." This gives you verbal permission to start a new habit of association that will lower your response to stress. The short prayer could be "Jesus, You are with me," the affirming word to yourself could be "I am a child of God" and then take a deep breath.

For example, if you're driving home from work and somebody cuts in front of you, respond to it with this new formula (prayer, affirming word, deep breath). No matter the stress, we can respond to it consistently with prayer, an affirming word to self, and a deep breath, it will help change our response to that stress.

We live in a society that continues to place too much emphasis on what we do for a living. When you meet someone and you share your name with them, what's usually the next question they ask you? "What do you do?" When I hear this I sometimes want to answer, "I don't care what I do, ask me who I am!" If we focus too much on what we do, we can end up with false understandings of who we are.

At this point, please turn back to page 15 and look at the stressors you indicated you partially control and those you can directly control. Now, spend a few minutes telling yourself, out loud if possible, "The next time I worry about _____, I'll say a prayer, tell myself an affirming word, and take a good breath from the diaphragm." Take time to do that for each worry you encounter. You'll be amazed at how effective it is.

On pages 85, 87, and 90 you'll find "Cut-Out Reminders." If you think it would be helpful, please cut out the two cards that say "New formula: STRESS = Prayer, Affirming Word, Deep Breath." I recommend putting one of these cards in your front pocket and the other in a place where you'll see it every day: in your day-planner, in your smart phone, on the mirror in your bathroom, or on your fridge.

Another association technique I like to teach concerns the color red. In our culture, we're taught early on the alarming effects of this color: red police lights, red fire trucks, red stop signs, red stop lights. But how would your life be different if you associated the color red with prayer and deep breathing? When we do this consistently we start to have a new response to the color red and our thoughts are more peaceful (from the prayer) and our bodies are calmer (from the deep breathing).

I taught this technique at a corporate workshop and the participants loved it. I heard back later that it was still working for them to lower their response to stress. That's because these association techniques work and are a tremendous gift from God.

Reflection Questions About Association Techniques

1) Of the association techniques offered in this chapter, which one do you like best?

2) How will practicing that technique today help you change your response to stress?

Prayer About Association Techniques

All good and ever loving God, you have created me in your freedom and for your freedom. Yet I tend to forget the freeing love you have for me when stress is high and anxiety lingers. Please send me your Spirit today so I can learn how to use association techniques. By using them I can learn how to change my response to stress around me and will open my heart to your freedom. Amen.

Strategy 5: You Are Not the Problem

"The Father has loved us so much that we are called children of God." —I John 3:1

We live in a society that places too much emphasis on what we do for a living. When you meet someone and you share your name with them, what's usually the next question they ask you? "What do you do?" When I hear this I sometimes want to answer, "I don't care what I do; ask me who I am!" If we focus too much on what we do, we can end up with a false understanding of who we are.

We all have false notions of who we are, and sometimes we can even think our actions create our identity. So when we make a mistake we can feel like a mistake. But that thinking is a mistake! In the Gospels when Jesus met a sincere person with an open heart, He never associated their actions with their identity. Jesus never made the person the problem when it came to repentant, open hearts.

If Jesus had associated people's actions (sometimes life-time actions) with their identity, there's no way Jesus would have forgiven the thief on the cross (Luke 23:43), Peter after his denial (John 21:15), the adulteress caught in sin (John 8:1-11), or anyone else He forgave. All of these parables point to a deep lesson about Christ's love for us: when it comes to a repentant heart, Jesus never equates what a person does with who the person is. We need to learn from Christ and do the same—beginning with ourselves.

If you tend to make this mistake, please take time to think about how this thought is probably increasing your stress and anxiety. We are not the problem; the Bible tells us we are children of God. Of course what we do, how we think, and the attitudes we have can be problematic, so we need to focus on those as we heal anxiety and stress.

When's the last time you told yourself the truth of who you are as a precious, powerful, and prayerful child of the King? Unfortunately, many of us don't do that daily. Do you? I think it's critical to start the daily habit of telling ourselves who we are as children of God. Create a plan today to begin to tell yourself at least three positive, Scripturally based truths about who you are.

This can help lower anxiety and stress because how we view ourselves has a tremendous impact on our stress levels, either positively or negatively. You may need to place this truth on your mirror in your bathroom, in your cell phone, on your refrigerator, in a journal, or any place you'll see it daily to remind yourself of your great identity.

If you come to our house you'll see a sign on our bathroom mirror that reads: "I am a child of God. Treat me accordingly." This little sign has helped lower my stress because

I no longer think of myself as the problem. If that could help you, go to the Cut-Out Reminders on page 87 and you'll find two copies of that little saying you can use.

When I'm awake enough, I love to use my daily shower to remind myself of my baptism. This helps me to remember that God has chosen me for a reason and a mission on this earth, and I am God's child. You're no different. God has great plans for you as well; you are His child. This truth needs to permeate all we do and all we think. Because we are children of the King we need to ask ourselves: are we treating ourselves like royalty? Many of us don't. We don't make time for ourselves to think about the goodness that God has given us because we feel that would be sinful. It's not a sin to recognize the mystery and gift that Psalm 8 proclaims: we are little less than gods. This isn't about pride; it's about thanking God for our identity in Christ and treating ourselves according to that identity.

Reflection Questions About You Are Not the Problem

1) If you feel like you're the problem, who taught you that? You weren't born that way; it's a learned behavior and can therefore be un-learned and healed.

2) Have you forgiven the person who taught you that you're the problem? (For more information on forgiveness, please see the next chapter, "Forgiveness Fundamentals.")

3) What actions can you do daily to remind yourself of your great identity as a child of God?

Prayer About You Are Not the Problem

Oh God, you created me in your image and likeness and redeemed me with your Son's life, death and resurrection. I am precious. You waited (so to speak) for me for a long time, and now I am on this earth and you delight in my life. Please send me your Holy Spirit today so that I may come to see clearly that I am not the problem but that I am your precious and powerful child. Amen.

Strategy 6: Forgiveness Fundamentals

"When you are praying, if you are angry with someone, *forgive him* so that your Father in heaven will also *forgive* your sins." —Mark 11:25

Learning and using forgiveness fundamentals are essential in managing our stress and anxiety. When we forgive someone, it lowers our stress and helps our body to heal. Unfortunately, in our society, there are many misunderstandings about forgiveness.

Recently, my wife and I were at a wedding where the pastor told the young couple that they need to learn how to "forgive and forget." I almost stood up and shouted, "Oh please, don't fill this young couple with that tripe." I'm not sure who coined the phrase "forgive and forget," but only God is fully capable of that, and even God forgives and redeems (brings good from it).

When it comes to understanding forgiveness it's good to understand that God made men and women differently. Women have larger hippocampi than men do. The hippocampus is a structure in the brain that's responsible for memory. Overall, women remember vividly (think theater-like, 3-D format). Compare that to the way most men remember, which is in much less detail (think black and white stick figures). I've heard this truth spoken from so many couples over the years as a coach and therapist. The conversation goes something like this: Wife: "Jim, I can't forget this thing he did (or said)." Husband: "Jim, I can't remember what she can't forget." Both have been correct. Think about the difference in brain chemistry the next time you hear "forgive and forget," and gently remind the person who said it that the statement isn't rooted in good biology. If we all do this, maybe that silly cliché will disappear.

Forgiveness is a paradox. Forgiveness is tricky; it's both a decision and a process. It's a decision because it involves using our will and intellect to decide to forgive. It's not a feeling; we need to decide to forgive. Jesus said, "you must forgive . . . 70 times seven" (Mt. 18:22). Jesus didn't say "You must feel like forgiving." Instead Jesus states that forgiveness is an act of the will and intellect.

Yet it's also a process because we have a right to work through the hurt with someone who is helpful and will validate our feelings (a pastor, a friend, a therapist). Don't wait to feel like you need to forgive because that may never happen. That said, if you have a very hard time forgiving a person, the first place to start is prayer: ask God for the grace to decide to forgive as you process the hurts with someone you trust.

To understand more completely the need for processing, recall the story where Peter denies Jesus. Peter was forgiven, but he needed to process those feelings of shame, hurt, and more with someone he trusted (see John chapter 21 for the story of Jesus and Peter on the seashore after the Resurrection). Jesus knew this was a need of Peter's, and He created a time where these feelings could be processed for healing. We need to do the same.

Forgiveness does not excuse. Forgiving someone does not, in any way, excuse the hurt that was done. It's a decision to let go of retribution and to allow God to begin to heal and restore the relationship, if that is what's needed. When we let go of the hurt, God can start to redeem it and bring good from it. If you choose to hold onto the hurt, be careful, because before you know it that hurt will start to hold onto you and nearly create a life of its own. So let go of the hurt through journaling and shredding, talking, and Christian therapy.

Forgiveness is not reconciliation. Reconciliation is about restoring the relationship to wholeness. Forgiveness may be the first step toward reconciliation, but sometimes if the person has died, or if it's not possible to have true reconciliation, forgiveness is still always a healing reality for the person who chooses to forgive. I have worked with many victims of abuse, and there's no intent to have reconciliation in those relationships. However, when the person who was abused is able to decide to forgive the abuser and starts to process the hurts, this opens the door to much healing. On the other hand, in a close relationship (marriage, friend, pastor, member of church) we may want reconciliation, so we need to begin with forgiveness as the first step toward possible reconciliation.

Forgiveness must be God-centered. If we focus on ourselves too much, we may never decide to forgive. During the forgiveness process we may need to grieve over the hurt that was done with someone we trust. That's good and healing. Remember that Christ cried when He grieved, so we can follow His lead. Tears can be healing. When we do grief work as Christians we ultimately know that the Holy Spirit can transform the grief into gratitude (for more on grieving, see the next chapter). I remember a couple who worked with me to heal an affair. They continue to report that the forgiveness that is happening has created a better marriage for them. The marriage will never be the same, I told them, but it can be so much better because God wants to bring new life from all of our "death" experiences, as long as we keep our forgiveness God-centered.

You have a right to your justified anger. However, you don't have a right to take that anger out on yourself or anyone else. Imagine an "anger bottle." Place all of your daily anger in your "anger bottle" and tell it that you'll get to it later that day. Then when you're able, set aside time to journal your anger out, talk it out, exercise it out, pray it out, etc. When you exercise and start to sweat, that's when you open up your "anger bottle" and let go of the anger and harness it. As a member of the Body of Christ you have dominion over your anger and your hurt. You own it and you use it for the good so that it doesn't own you.

Practice forgiveness. In order to forgive, there must first be a decision to forgive. If you can't make a decision to forgive right now, this prayer said a few times a day can be helpful: "Oh God, give me the grace to decide to forgive_____ and give me the grace to work through the hurt that _____ has caused." This prayer will help you to eventually decide to forgive. In the meantime, start working through the hurts. You can do this by journaling or by talking about the hurt to several safe people, such as a pastor, a good friend, or a Christian therapist.

Use rituals to forgive and heal. Rituals create an atmosphere where people can heal. Many rituals in worship and healing were used in the Old Testament, and Jesus also used rituals to heal. In the Gospel of John, chapter 6, Jesus uses ritual to multiply the little boy's loaves and fish. Later in the Gospel of John, Jesus uses another ritual to heal the blind man (John 9:6). We can use ritual, as well, to heal and forgive. Many individuals and couples love to privately write down all of their hurts and then safely burn the paper. If you do this, watch the ritual. The ash is a different substance than the paper (a chemical change). And ash can be used as a fertilizer! This is exactly what God wants to do with our hurts as well. Romans 8:28 promises us that God will turn our hurts into good when we love God. But, in order for that healing to happen, we need to give our hurts to God. If we hold onto our hurts too tightly, God respects our free will and may not transform them into the abundant life God wants for us.

Say the words "I forgive you." If you say to a co-worker or a loved one, "I'm sorry about that," what's usually their next response? "It's OK." This isn't a good practice for forgiveness because it invalidates the whole apology. It isn't OK, because someone was hurt. The next time someone apologizes to you, say, "I forgive you." Or, if you can't decide to forgive at that time, say "Thanks for the thoughtful words." Then, work through the hurt with someone you trust and later decide to forgive the person.

Learn to forgive yourself. My best friend and soulmate taught me this years ago (thanks, Maureen). I asked her to forgive me and she did. Then, she looked at me and asked, "Do you forgive yourself?" I hadn't thought about that but it sounded really good. Since then I have made it a habit (most of the time) to forgive myself. After I ask

God for forgiveness, I like to put my hand on my heart and say, "I forgive you, Jim." This has been a wonderfully freeing ritual for me and many others, all thanks to the Lord, working through my wife.

When the offender doesn't say "Sorry." Again, work through the hurt and pray for the grace to forgive. The Lord will give you the grace eventually to decide to forgive even when the person doesn't say they are sorry, or can't do so because of death or disability. Forgive the person and it will help your physical, spiritual, emotional, and relational health. When we see that Jesus forgave those who crucified Him and they didn't ask for forgiveness, it can help us to forgive when the offender doesn't apologize.

Reflection Questions About Forgiveness Fundamentals

1) Are there any forgiveness issues you need to work through? What are they and how will it help your stress to work through them?

2) How will practicing the forgiveness fundamentals help lower your stress and/or anxiety?

Prayer About Forgiveness Fundamentals

All good and forgiving God, you love me so very much that through your Son you continue to forgive me every time I need your compassion and turn to you. Thank you for your mercy and forgiveness. Please send your Holy Spirit into my heart today so that I may imitate your love and learn to forgive myself and others. Amen.

Strategy 7: Identify and Work Through Grief Issues via Romans 8:28

"We know that in everything God works for the good of those who love him."
—Romans 8:28

Typically, when we hear the phrase "grief issues" we think about grief after a physical death. Death is certainly a powerful grief issue. But what about the other grief issues that we all have in our lives: a friend moving, a word or phrase that was spoken, negative words we tell ourselves, a lost opportunity, a sad anniversary date? There are so many of these grief areas in our lives. Yet, as Christians we also know the power of Christ. Through Christ's life, death, resurrection and sending of the Holy Spirit, death and all of its consequences, especially our grief issues, have been re-ordered, re-structured, and redeemed. Two thousand years ago Saint Paul, in his deeply theological letter to the Christian community in Rome, wrote about this truth in Romans 8:28. This verse is the reason I get out of bed in the morning. It summarizes the entire Scriptures. It's a mystery that gives us all hope: God will bring good from everything we go through as long as we love God.

I remember working with Tim. He hadn't taken time to name his grief issues before we met. He liked what I was teaching him as his Christian coach: that we don't productively grow until we productively grieve. When he started that process of naming his grief issues and productively working through them through Romans 8:28, it made a huge difference in his life. People started noticing that he had more energy and was more at peace. That's the fruit of productive grieving, because un-named grieving can produce more stress. We want to work productively through our grief issues, like Tim did, so they don't destructively work through us. A good place to start this grief work is by identifying our grief issues and then spending time productively grieving them and giving them to God, who wants to bring good from them (Romans 8:28).

For example, my mother died from breast cancer in 1995. We were very close and I can still hear her laugh. I grieved her death as best I could and God now brings people into my life who have also lost parents and other loved ones. Because of the Holy Spirit, I can console others with the same consolations that God has given me (Second Corinthians 1). That's the resurrection cycle, and it's balm to grieving. It's amazing and healing to understand that God loves us so much that the Holy Spirit desires to bring good from every pain we go through.

Our culture doesn't see that truth and therefore, we don't grieve well as a society. We either maximize or minimize the hurt. The invitation is to find balance and take time to feel the hurt and experience the healing that comes with the grief process.

When we grieve, we need to do so as Christians. We need to recognize that the Holy Spirit will transform our grief into gratitude, but that takes time, energy, and relationship. The hurt happened in relationship, so the healing will happen in relationship. Our Lord remembers and redeems the grief process so we know that all the grief areas in our life—whether they're large or small—will lead to new life when we take time to grieve them and give them to God.

We all grieve differently. Some need to make time to cry, look at photos, or remember words and phrases. Others need less time. There's no one correct way to grieve. The key is to focus on how God wants to heal and bring good from it. If you or a loved one feel like you're getting stuck in your grief, it may be an indicator that you need some other type of help working through these areas, such as coaching or counseling. When we work productively through our daily grief issues, we can typically become less stuck in the grieving process.

Reflection Questions About Grieving Through Romans 8:28

1) Are there any grief areas in your life (big or small)? Take time to write them out (i.e. name them)

2) Romans 8:28 reminds us that God wants to bring good from all of our hurts. How will grieving with this verse change your grieving? How will it lower your stress levels?

Prayer About Grieving Through Romans 8:28

All good and compassionate God, you understand my need to grieve. Through your Son, Jesus Christ our Lord, you have redeemed the entire grief process. I ask that you please send me your Holy Spirit. May your Spirit help me to name the grief issues in my life so that your love can help me work productively through them. I pray this through Christ our Lord and in the power of the Holy Spirit. Amen.

Strategy 8: The Power of Water and Oil

"The sweet smells of perfume and oils is pleasant. . . ." —Proverbs 27:9

Water was used as an ancient symbol of freedom for the Israelites after they were led through the Red Sea by Moses. In the New Testament, Jesus was baptized in the River Jordan. Water is still used in our churches today as a symbol of cleansing and power, especially in baptism. Throughout the entire Scriptures, oil was used to heal and anoint. Water and oil are excellent physical reminders of God's healing power and we need to apply these two potent symbols in the healing of anxiety as well.

I worked with a man named Chad, whose anxiety was very high. He started using some of the recommendations in this workbook. Some of them helped lower his anxiety levels, but something was still missing. We figured out that he wasn't taking time to utilize water and oil in his life. When I asked him if he ever used the bath to relax, he answered "No Jim, my wife takes a bath every night to help with her stress, but I never have." I think he heard the irony of his words. His wife was using the bath to help with her stress but he didn't do the same.

Here's what I told Chad: Buy two small bottles of lavender essential oil, or any calming oil you like. You can buy these oils online or in the organic section of your local grocery store. Essential oils have been used for thousands of years and lavender oil is used to bring calm and tranquility. The sense of smell is one of the most powerful memory conductors in the brain and when it's used in conjunction with the tranquil effect of a bath and oil, it will create a sense of peace and relaxation.

The next time you take a relaxing bath, with soft music and maybe a candle or two, take out the first bottle of lavender oil and smell it. Focus on the warm water, the soothing calming scent of the oil, and the love that Christ has for you. Try to make time for this four times a week, or every day if you can, and the brain will start to create a very relaxing memory with the smell of the oil.

Next, keep the second bottle in a place you know is going to be stressful (the car, school, office, etc.). Or, keep a small bottle with you in your pocket or purse. Whenever you encounter a stressful situation, take out the lavender oil and smell it by taking a slow, deep breath. Your brain, which has been trained to associate the scent of lavender oil with a warm relaxing bath, will start to calm down and you'll remember the relaxation of your bath time.

I explained this to Chad and he was eager for more healing, so he practiced this recommendation and started taking relaxing baths. He also bought some lavender oil and used it during his bath times. He reports that he has been using the oil especially at stressful times with his job and it has really helped to lower his stress response. That's because he has trained his brain to respond in a calming way to lavender.

Reflection Questions About the Power of Water and Oil

1) Do you need to start making time for a relaxing bath? If so, have you used the lavender oil association?

2) How will this association help lower your stress in the next few weeks?

Prayer About the Peace-filled Gift of Water and Oil

Oh God of love, you have created me with the ability to remember calming thoughts and scents. Please send me your Spirit today as I want to learn to use oil and water to change my stress response to a more peaceful experience of your power and love. I make this prayer through Christ our Lord and in the power of your Holy Spirit. Amen.

Strategy 9: Understand the Pros and Cons of Your Image of God

". . . the glory of Christ, who is exactly like God." —II Corinthians 4:4

How do you view God? Many of us don't stop to think about this question very often. Yet it's essential when discussing stress and anxiety management. Here are a few ground rules when doing image of God work:

1) **There are rarely neutral images of God** (i.e. the majority of our images are either positive or negative).

2) **All of our images of God will somehow be incomplete on this earth**. This is because God's ways are not our ways, and yet Jesus loves us with an intimate, personal love. God is an ultimate mystery, yet is revealed in the Person of Jesus Christ. As humans, all of our images of God will somehow be incomplete.

3) **Our image of God helps or hinders our stress and anxiety**. If our primary image of God is one of total judge who "waits to catch us messing up," this will increase stress hormones and blood pressure. If, on the other hand, our primary image of God is one of lover who seeks us out (e.g., the Book of Hosea, the Song of Solomon, and many other places in the Bible), this will have a dramatic impact on our day-to-day peace.

One client I worked with is Tami. She shared with me that her primary image of God was very negative. We discussed how her image of God was directly linked to her anxiety, and we started to work on balancing out this image of God. When we were able to formulate healthier images of God, she started to feel better about herself. Indeed, this takes time, but Tami has begun to honestly assess what her primary image of God is and how it affects her stress and anxiety levels.

So what about you? What's your primary image of God? Take a moment now to write some words that best describe the major way you view God to be in relationship with you:

Now take a look at that list. Is it mostly positive? Mostly negative? A combination of both? Take some time today to pray about your primary image of God and how it relates to your stress levels.

For example, if most of your list is negative, it could be helpful to pray with and understand the following Scripture passages, because they can start to heal your negative images of God, which can then lessen your stress levels. Pray with these images and memorize them. If you need a copy of these to cut out, you'll find them on the "Cut-out Reminders" page at the back of the workbook.

+ "I am God's child" (Romans 8:16).
+ "The Father loves me so much that I am a child of God" (I John 3:1).
+ "Don't be afraid, because I have saved you. I have called you by name, and you are mine" (Isaiah 43:1).
+ "No one will be able to defeat you all your life. Just as I was with Moses, so I will be with you. I will not leave you or forget you" (Joshua 1:5).
+ "Like babies you will be nursed and held in my arms and bounced on my knees. I will comfort you as a mother comforts her child" (Isaiah 66:12-13).
+ "I leave you peace; my peace I give you . . . So don't let your hearts be troubled or afraid" (John 14:27).

Reflection Questions About Your Primary Image of God

1) How will you practice a healthier image of God today?

2) How will this practice help lower your response to stress today?

Prayer About Your Primary Image of God

God of love, I adore you. I thank you for your Son and your Holy Spirit. Although I will never be able to fully understand you, it helps me to name how I imagine you to be. If I have any negative images of you, please heal them. You love me. I'm your child. Please send me your Holy Spirit today so I can see and eventually feel the powerful and cleansing love that you have for me. Amen.

Strategy 10: The School of Stress

"You meant to hurt me, but God turned your evil into good . . ."
—Genesis 50:20

It may seem completely counter-intuitive, and maybe even a little ridiculous, but believe it or not, our stress, and even anxiety, might have a profound lesson to teach us. This is the school of stress. Often, stress and anxiety are trying to teach us something very important. For example, they may be telling us that we need more sleep, more recreation time, or more downtime.

For example, when my wife and I suffered with infertility early in our marriage, and eventually several miscarriages, I had high anxiety. This is when I was diagnosed with anxiety. When I examined what that anxiety was telling me, I found out it was saying that I needed to have more authentic time and space to grieve, more exercise time, and more prayer time as well. When I tended to these needs, the anxiety became more manageable.

To consider that my stress could actually teach me something was eye-opening, and it has helped me even to this day. So now when I feel that familiar tightness in my chest, I try to pray and think about what's going on in my life. I may have to ask my wife, spiritual director, or close Christian brother about it and ask if they can help me name what's going on. So often the stress and anxiety happens in relationship, so the healing will happen in relationship as well. We need each other in the Body of Christ, and I rely on others speaking truths into my life to help me sort out what my stress is trying to teach me.

Reflection Questions About the School of Stress

1) What is your stress and anxiety telling you? Take a moment to think about what your stress could be trying to tell you and write it down:

2) What do you need to do today based on this lesson from the "School of Stress"?

Prayer About Understanding the School of Stress

Oh God of wisdom, in your love, nothing is wasted. Even the stress and anxiety in my life can teach me something. Touch my ears and my eyes so that I can clearly hear and see what lessons I need to learn from them. Open my mind to your Spirit, who continues to use so many ways to teach me about your love. Amen.

Strategy 11: Navigate Wisely Those People Whose Actions Increase Your Stress

". . . test the spirits to see if they are from God." —I John 4:1

My parents taught me to avoid being around people whose actions stress me out. That's common sense, and a lesson we can all benefit from. As an adult I understand it this way: if I'm around people whose attitudes and actions don't help me become more of a son of God, I give myself permission to not be around them. It just makes good sense from a boundary point of view.

Of course, this boundary issue doesn't include reaching out to people who are open to the Gospel message of freedom in Christ. We need to be instruments of God to build the Kingdom and to reach non-believers as well as believers. But when there are people in our lives who consistently don't act like Christians and who actually cause too much stress in our lives, I think it's a holy idea to be smart about navigating this source of stress. If you feel this is a good friendship, you have a right to talk to your friend about their offensive actions. If you do that and they still choose not to change their actions, you can approach them with a friend (following Matthew 18:17).

If their actions still stink, you can give yourself permission to move on if you feel the Spirit is telling you that would be a smart decision. Even Christ himself told us to ". . . be as smart as snakes and as innocent as doves" (Matthew 10:16). And Psalm 101 has ancient wisdom: "I will hate those who turn against you; they will not be found near me. Let those who want to do wrong stay away from me; I will have nothing to do with evil." These statements don't pull any punches. The idea of creating this type of boundary is very counter-cultural.

If that source of stress is family, it's a little trickier. A cleansing ritual shower or bath and plenty of time alone before or during the visit can be helpful in these cases. Creating "safe spaces" during the visit can also be helpful, whether they're daily walks, visits to churches, or visiting other friends. These strategies can help if you find yourself in difficult dynamics with in-laws or family when you have to be around them.

I saw this in-law dynamic with John and Sue. They sought me out for marriage counseling, but it didn't take long to see that a major source of their stress was from his parents' attitudes and actions. That doesn't mean John's parents were the problem; their actions and attitudes were, and they led to much stress in the marriage. I like to tell people in this situation that Sue didn't marry John's parents—she married John!

The Bible talks about how "a man will leave his father and mother and be united with his wife, and the two will become one body" (Genesis 2: 24). Unfortunately, this leaving and cleaving doesn't always happen. It's a sad dynamic that can be addressed by setting new boundaries and giving ourselves permission to listen to Christ and be smart about navigating this stress. Being around John's parents was so stressful for John and Sue that they "started to worry about Christmas in October" because they "had" to go to John's house for Christmas. We discussed how this type of worry is avoidable if they give themselves permission to not go to his parents' house over Christmas. The last time I checked, Christmas is not about fake smiles and drinking alcohol. Christmas is about the mystery of the incarnation and redemption: how God desired to become one of us so that we could become more like God. John and Sue liked this idea and gave themselves permission to not go to the places of stress. They had a much more relaxed celebration of the Christ-child and His love for humanity.

Reflection Questions About Avoiding Others' Toxic Attitudes and Actions

1) Are there people in your life whose actions and attitudes don't help you become more of who you are as a precious child of God? Take time to list some of the things they say and do that you need to avoid:

2) What is God calling you to do about this relationship?

3) If this is an in-law situation, is your spouse open to the wisdom in this chapter? If not, how can you still visit with your in-laws and create a less stressful situation?

Prayer About Avoiding Others' Toxic Attitudes and Actions

Oh good and loving God, you desire that we create healthy and holy relationships with each other. Send me your Spirit of wisdom and discernment so that I am able to name actions that are not holy, and give me your strength to be smart about what I am called to do with tricky situations. Send people into my life who will help me see the truth that I do not have to expose myself to actions that are toxic. I pray this through Christ our Lord and in the power of the Holy Spirit. Amen.

Strategy 12: Enter into Daily Sabbath Moments

"Come away by yourselves, and we will go to a lonely place to get some rest."
—Mark 6:31

While living in Israel, I was struck by how serious many of the Jewish people are about the Sabbath. What a great lesson in life, and one that is badly needed in America. I remember trying to get home as quickly as possible on Friday nights because the city bus system in Jerusalem stops at sun down to honor the Jewish Sabbath on Saturday. It made me ponder how as a child growing up in Verndale, Minnesota (a village of 540 people), there was only one place open on Sunday: the local restaurant, which served brunch after church. I think we have lost the re-creational power of the Sabbath in our hectic, productive-centered culture. We need to learn how to enter into daily and weekly Sabbath moments.

Daily Sabbath moments are probably best used during those times throughout our work day when we become fatigued, frazzled, or fearful and we need a little break. This chapter discusses five daily Sabbath suggestions that can be helpful for you today.

The first daily Sabbath moment is recognizing the "holiness of the humdrum" through prayer. We read in I Cor. 10:3, Col. 3:17, and other Scripture verses that whatever we do, we are to do it for the glory of God. When we are actively in prayer throughout the day it can remind us of who we are (God's children) and of how much God loves us and wants us to lift up everything as a prayer.

So before you sit down to catch up on your emails, say a prayer for those you're emailing. When you're in a meeting and getting overwhelmed, bored, or uncomfortable, pray for people who are unemployed or under-employed. When at home changing a diaper, doing laundry, or cleaning the kitchen—for the fifth time that day—pray for those who don't have clean water or soap. All of these examples are instances of the "miracle of the mundane" and are powerful invitations to enter into this daily Sabbath moment.

The second daily Sabbath moment is to create and use a "peace place." It may be the mountains, it may be a church. It might be nature or a lake, or Grandma's house where the aroma of cookies is in the air. It might be sipping tea with a friend or the shores of Ireland. No matter where the place is, it's an excellent way to enter into a daily Sabbath moment for even five minutes.

There are a few steps needed to "create" a peace place before you can "go" there. First, remember a place where you have visited (ideally) that was good, safe, welcoming, and full of peace. Typically our peace places will be areas that we have physically visited. However, I think it could work to use a place that you haven't visited if you need to; this would simply take more imagination. The following are areas that may work for your "peace place:"

The next step for creating your "peace place" is to use all five of your physical senses to really experience it. See the sights, feel the wind, hear the sounds, etc. Don't stop at the physical senses when creating your peace place; also get in touch with your emotional responses about the place: calm, peace, love, joy, etc. Sometimes your mental pictures of the place can help replicate your physical and emotional senses of it.

The final step to create your "peace place" is to let yourself know that you are "going" there. Once you "go" there, enjoy it and relax. When alone, you can even say "I need to go to my peace place for five minutes right now." This verbal permission can be a very effective way of getting your mind, body, and soul ready for your imagination to transport you to your peace place. Once there, feel your blood pressure lower, feel your muscles loosen, and experience the calming memories that you have.

Practice these three steps until you're comfortable going to your peace place. Then, when you feel that stress is high, or you feel you need a Sabbath moment, use your imagination and take yourself there for a few minutes of rest.

The third daily Sabbath moment is self-massage. Self massages of the neck, shoulders, and forehead can be very relaxing and can lower stress. I recommend doing this every hour or so for five minutes when you're stuck at a desk for several hours. Jesus used touch often because touch heals.

The fourth daily Sabbath moment is to train your body to recognize the difference between tight muscles and relaxed muscles. This is a powerful exercise when done consistently and can be a great four or five minute daily Sabbath moment. Here's how it works:

Start with the top of your body and work your way down by first tightening the muscles and then relaxing them. I like to start with the forehead. Make a frown and tighten those forehead muscles, feel the tension and hold for five seconds or so. Then, release those muscles and give yourself permission to keep them relaxed. Many of us tighten these forehead muscles all day long, and it can lead to increased stress, anxiety, and even headaches. Once you have tightened and relaxed the forehead muscles, go to the nose, lips, and cheek muscles: again, purse your lips tight, crinkle your nose and create tension; hold it for about five seconds, then let the relaxation come. Feel the difference between the tension and relaxation. Then, progress to your neck, shoulders, abs, thighs, calves, feet and toes with the same tighten-relax muscle response.

Ideally, throughout the day if we feel our muscles tighten, we should try to relax them as quickly as possible. This type of training can help us stay aware of how tight our muscles are and to try to relax them as soon as we feel them tightening.

The fifth daily Sabbath moment that is catching on well is the "lunch-time walk." When I worked as a hospital chaplain we would use some of our lunch time to walk the stairs on bad weather days, or go outside when the weather was good. This type of physical activity is truly re-creative and can be a wonderful daily Sabbath moment.

Reflection Questions About Creating Daily Sabbath Moments

1) Of the daily Sabbath moments listed, which one do you think will help you lower your stress throughout the day?

2) When do you want to start practicing that daily Sabbath moment?

Prayer About Creating Daily Sabbath Moments

Oh God of the Sabbath, you give rest to the weary and peace to the worker. You did not create us to work continually. Send your Spirit into our hearts today so we can start to practice daily Sabbath moments in order to enter more fully into the rest and peace you have planned for us. Amen.

Strategy 13: Christian Meditation

". . . I consider everything you have done. I think about all you have made."
—Psalm 143:5

I remember working with Lucy. Like so many of us, she wrestled with high anxiety. When I asked her during one of our sessions if she had practiced Christian meditation, she looked at me as though I said something scandalous: "Christian meditation." She told me "Jim, when I hear the word meditation I think about the 70s and about many things that have nothing to do with the Lord." I thanked her for her response, and we had a good conversation about what true "Christian meditation" is.

I told Lucy that in the Psalms the word "meditate" is used about 12 times. The book of Psalms would have been memorized and prayerfully recited by our Lord Jesus 2,000 years ago. I'm convinced that Jesus meditated on God's love and law as the Psalms teach us. I'm also convinced that when we follow our Lord's example and meditate on God's love for us, our stress and anxiety levels will lower. After I explained this to Lucy, she asked, "How do I get started?"

First, you need a quiet spot and a slower pace. If you're new to Christian meditation it may be helpful to have a clock so you can keep track of the time. Some like to set the alarm for three minutes or so, but others find it too jarring and would rather just keep an eye on the time. I recommend starting slowly—a few minutes at a time—and see how it goes. As for the quiet space that's needed: I sometimes choose a church, a quiet spot in the house after the kids go to bed (instead of watching TV or surfing the net), or a quiet place at work, if you're blessed to have one.

Second, select a word or phrase from the Scriptures that speaks peace into your life. I like to meditate on the name "Jesus" because "every knee will bow to the name of Jesus..." (Philippians 2:10). I love the notion that every knee must bow! That includes the very strong "knees" of my anxiety at times; it has no choice but to humbly bow as I meditate on the Holy Name. Choose whichever scriptural word or phrase works for you. Some choose "peace," "I am precious," or "I am loved." Other ideas: "In Jesus I am healing," "In Christ I am safe," "I am God's son/daughter," and "I am more than victorious."

Once you're in your quiet space and you have chosen your word or phrase, you need to get into a comfortable position, but not so comfy that you fall asleep . . . meditation is not hibernation. Once you're comfortable, start to say your word or phrase softly to yourself—or even gently audibly if that helps and you're alone. Say it slowly and let your word or phrase sink deep within yourself, permeating all you are.

I can almost guarantee that once we slow down to this pace our minds will flood with thoughts, worries, concerns of the day or year, and memories. It seems that in our brokenness we have a very hard time being still and knowing that God is God. Don't worry about that very typical response. The good news is that the more you meditate, the quieter your mind and thought processes can become. There are some points to remember when you start slowing down and the thoughts burst in. Adopt a semi-passive attitude toward those incoming thoughts and continue to repeat your focus word or phrase. Also recognize that for all practical purposes most incoming thoughts fit into two categories. The first category is neutral thoughts (bills to pay, kids to feed, taking the dog to the vet, etc.). These are normal thoughts that threaten to distract us. The second category can be temptations (i.e. temptations to think something uncharitable, to say something unkind, to judge someone unjustly). I believe in spiritual warfare, although we need to understand the fight is won and all we have to do is to say "yes" to the victory.

Now, let's talk about applying a semi-passive attitude to the two categories of thoughts that can be present when we slow down. For the first category, the neutral thoughts, it's important not to fight them. Instead, a semi-passive attitude recognizes that they are there and then immediately goes back to repeating the focus word or phrase. I call it a semi-passive attitude because if the thought is a blatant temptation (the second category of thoughts) it's good to simply rebuke that temptation, say no to it, and then go back to the word or phrase. An example may help illustrate.

The other day I was meditating in one of my favorite quiet spots, a local church. When I started to repeat my word or phrase ("Jesus") I was distracted by a neutral thought (something about work, if I recall), so I simply recognized the thought and then went back to meditating. I think I said something like, "Yep, I know you're here, but I'm thinking about Jesus right now." That helped me calm down and focus more on my point of meditation, the powerful name of Jesus. During that same meditation time I was tempted to think an uncharitable thought. All I did with the temptation was to say, "No, I'm meditating on the name of Jesus."

The more meditation you practice, the easier this process becomes. It's like riding a bike, playing an instrument, or driving a car. If you listed all the steps needed to learn how to ride a bike, it would probably surprise and intimidate you. But once you ride a bike you don't even think about the mechanics of what you're doing, you simply do it. Christian meditation is similar. Practice it and when you do it properly it's amazing for reducing anxiety and managing stress. Ideally it's good to practice this technique for at least 10 to 20 minutes a day. If you have never done it, start out with about two or three minutes and try it. Then, add to that timeframe.

I have witnessed many people who had high anxiety learn that Christian meditation will lower stress and anxiety. Lucy, the woman from the start of this chapter, is one of them. She learned how to meditate and told me that it was very helpful in lowering her anxiety. I know firsthand that Christian meditation kills stress and anxiety.

Reflection Questions About Christian Meditation

1) Have you tried Christian meditation?

2) If not, what's stopping you from trying it?

3) After trying it for a few days, take time to write down how it's helped you lower your stress:

I invite you to read this list over and over again. It helps to see the victories that the Lord sends us, and Christian meditation is one of those victories.

Prayer About Christian Meditation

"Be still and know that I am God," *says the psalmist. Help me to understand the wisdom that silence is your first language, God. Send me your Holy Spirit to slow down my pace of life and to create sacred space and time for the practice of Christian meditation. I ask this through Christ, your Son, and in the power of your Holy Spirit. Amen.*

Strategy 14: Name and Tame Emotional Illusions

"Jesus answered, 'I am the way and the truth and the life.'" —John 14:6

Emotional illusions are rampant in our world and they usually either create or fuel our stress and anxiety. These tricky dynamics are much like optical illusions because optical illusions look real but aren't true. Emotional illusions feel real, but aren't true.

Think about one of my favorite natural optical illusions for a minute: water up ahead on the road. Most of us have seen this illusion that nature provides through heat waves and light bouncing off our optic nerve. When you see this illusion you would bet good money there's water up ahead: it looks real. But upon further thought and movement (it takes both to uncover any illusion) it's revealed that there's no water! Emotional illusions are the same, but instead of looking real, they *feel* real. And, like an optical illusion, it takes thought and movement to discover what's true.

Once this strategy is introduced and used it can create new ways of healing in our lives. The healing is powerful and sustaining because naming and taming emotional illusions isn't an attempt to ignore, repress, or suppress the feelings; this approach allows the feelings to be felt and then help the person think about the feelings and move through them to eventually ask one critical question, "Is this a true feeling?" Often, we need the Lord to provide someone to help us think and move to the answer, just like the Lord did for Bruce.

Bruce sought me out for counseling, and we worked hard on identifying his emotional illusions. Like all of us, he had many illusions in his life, but the primary one he wrestled with was the feeling that he was going to kill himself. You see, Bruce had a loved one who committed suicide and this emotional illusion was very strong in Bruce's life. He felt that because suicide had happened in his family, he was almost "destined" for a similar fate. The Holy Spirit blessed his hard work, and he did a great job in therapy. He was eventually able to move through the feeling and to the truth. As we did this movement together, he began to see that this was a real feeling that he didn't have to hide or feel ashamed about. He needed to talk about it with a trusted guest in his life, and he needed to pray about the fact that although it was a real feeling, it wasn't true.

We talked about how Bruce was dealing with things in his life compared to how his loved one who committed suicide dealt with things. This exercise helped him sort out how Bruce was making different choices than his loved one and therefore he didn't have to come to the same tragic ending. The movement of focusing on how his responses differed from his loved one's shed truth onto Bruce's emotional illusion. And like any illusion, when it's bathed in the light of truth, it can't continue. He let me pray with him, and for him. Our prayers frequently focused on how the truth will set Bruce free, and it will set us all free (John 8:31-31).

Now, thanks to God's healing power, Bruce is freed from this wicked emotional illusion. In fact, the last time I asked about it, he told me that it isn't even a possibility. That's the power of naming and taming emotional illusions.

Reflection Questions About Emotional Illusions

1) Have you named any emotional illusions in your life? If so, which ones?

2) How can the truth set you free from those emotional illusions?

3) If needed, do you have a reliable person you can trust with this illusion? If so, who is it, and when will you do that?

Prayer About Naming and Taming Emotional Illusions

Oh God, you give us the truth to set us free through your son Jesus Christ, our Lord. Please help me to see any emotional illusions in my life. Send me your Spirit so that I may see what I need to do in order to heal and bring to the truth these illusions without denying or repressing the feelings. It is your truth I seek, and your truth that sets me free. Amen.

Strategy 15: Identity is More Important Than Personality

"If anyone belongs to Christ, there is a new creation. The old things have gone; everything is made new!" —II Corinthians 5:17

"I'm a worrier," Jenny said with conviction during one of our early counseling sessions. I've heard this from many stressed out and anxious folks over the years, and Jenny was one of them. She truly believed that because she's a "type A" personality, she's therefore doomed to live a short life and die of a stress-induced heart attack at a young age. Jenny is not alone. There are many people who believe that they are worriers. In other words, they have *become* their symptoms of stress or worry. This belief only serves to perpetuate the very stress and anxiety they are trying to alleviate. So what can be done? A truth-based conversation about how identity is more important than personality is a great place to start.

There are many personality inventories out there that attempt to shed light on why people do what they do and how people can interact more productively together in professional and personal relationships. These may be helpful if used appropriately, but all too often they can be used as a convenient excuse to not become all God wants us to be. So in listening to people as a coach and a therapist I hear things like, "That's just the way I am," "I'm a worrier," "I'm an intellectual and feelings are not logical," or the most difficult to hear, "This is the way God made me." Many of us would simply like to rest on our personality traits, or many of us truly believe, as Jenny did, that we can't change our responses because "I have always been this way." I respectfully disagree.

What I told Jenny is the same thing I've told many people over the years: identity is more important than personality. *Personality* is important and comes from a mysterious combination of our natural birth and the environment in which we are raised. But *identity* comes from our supernatural birth seen in the Gospel of John 3:5: "Truly, truly, I say to you, unless one is born of water and the Spirit he cannot enter into the Kingdom of God." When we say "yes" to Christ's transforming love we are literally re-created, or re-born. We become a new person in Christ. As Gal. 2:19 says, "I have been crucified with Christ, and the life I live now is not my own; Christ is living in me. I still live my human life, but it is a life of faith in the Son of God, who loved me and gave himself for me." To be "crucified with Christ" means that we continue to open up our hearts to the power of the Holy Spirit so that we can daily die to ourselves, and therefore allow the Spirit to resurrect us daily. In this process we become more of who we are in our identity in Christ. This, of course, is a process and takes time, truth, trusted loved ones, and patience with ourselves. When we begin to see that our identity in Christ is more important than our personality, then we're able to start changing the false notions we send ourselves, such as "I'm a worrier" and "That's just the way I am."

And that's what Jenny now does in her life. Every time she catches herself repeating the lie "I'm a worrier," she tries to correct it by saying something like, "I belong to Christ, and I feel worried about_____." This may seem like a small change, but for those of us struggling with stress and anxiety, it's huge! Jenny has told me that she now feels less stressed out and less anxious, and much of that is because she no longer believes she's a worrier. Instead, she's beginning to believe that she is sharing in Christ's identity and she sometimes feels worried about certain situations.

Reflection Questions About Your Great Identity

1) Do you, like many of us, place too much importance on personality or use it as an excuse to not become all of who God wants you to be?

2) If so, what can you do to help stop that so you can become free to be who you are as one who belongs to Christ?

Prayer About Your Identity in Christ

All loving God, through Christ your Son you have re-created me and have given me the gift of eternal life. Send your Holy Spirit into my heart today so that I will no longer come up with excuses to not become all you want me to be. I ask this through Christ our Lord and in the power of the Holy Spirit. Amen.

Strategy 16: Listen to the Word, Not to the Wounds

"God's word is alive and working and is sharper than a doubled-edged sword."
—Hebrews 4:12

Unfortunately, in our fallen world, wounds are everywhere. As Christians we believe there were no wounds before the fall of Adam and Eve. Wounds are a product of sin and God didn't create sin. However, in His perfect plan, God sent his Son, in the fullness of time, to redeem sin and therefore to redeem all the wounds we will ever endure. Jesus showed His wounds to his disciples after His resurrection, and thus transformed all the wounds of the world! Jesus could have chosen to let the resurrection erase His wounds completely, but He didn't. Instead, He transformed His wounds by the resurrection. By His power Jesus led His wounds from "gory" to "glory," and He wants us to do the same.

Because we belong to Christ (see the last strategy), we can say with confidence that every wound that has been inflicted upon us has already been redeemed! That's because we belong to Christ, and so we share in His very identity. We share in His resurrection power, as well. Therefore, our wounds have been resurrected by the resurrection of Christ. Of course our wounds still need to be tended, validated, and cared for. But in our Savior we have One who knows, heals, and redeems wounds. This means that there's great healing and hope when we listen to the Word (of God) and not to our wounds (not from God).

I remember this transformation of wounds with Linda. She told me that her first memory was being thrown across the room by a physically abusive parent. That's a huge, powerful wound and it tried to give Linda a false "identity" by "reminding" her that she's no good, she's not worthy of love, and she doesn't deserve to be treated respectfully. This is the power of wounds in life and we all have them, whether they're brutal, like Linda's, or less severe, like emotional neglect or yelling from a parent.

Linda eventually married an abusive husband because she unconsciously listened to her wounds. That's when I met her. We worked for years to help her listen less to those wounds. We also worked on the idea of her being able to prayerfully unite her wounds to the wounds of Christ every time she felt them, because when we do this, resurrection is guaranteed. Many Christians find it helpful to say a simple prayer when they feel the wound of stress or anxiety, something like: "Jesus, I unite this to your wounds and I know you can raise it to new life." It's Peter who reminds us that "By His wounds we are healed" (I Pet. 2:24). Again, this takes time and relationship. The wounds happened in a negative relationship and so often the healing will happen in a positive relationship, such as with a pastor or a Christian therapist.

After years of learning, Linda is now re-married and is doing much better, although when stress is high she still sometimes believes she's that little girl who doesn't deserve love—all because of listening to her wounds. But by listening daily to the Word of God and others who support that Word, there has been healing in Linda's life. Linda's story, to some degree, is also our story.

We all have hurts and wounds in our past or present. These wounds want us to listen to them and follow them. Because this advice is from a wound, it will lead us to some ugly places and can influence our major decisions. In Linda's case, she married an abusive husband because she had been listening to the wounds from her family of origin and following them for years. Our task is to rebuke the lie and to focus on the truth of the Word of God. This takes time and trusted individuals in our lives. But it's possible to heal, and the more we focus on that possibility, the more of a reality it becomes.

Reflection Questions About Listening to the Word, Not to the Wounds

1) Have you been able to identify wounds in your life? If so, have you been able to understand the consequences of "listening" to those wounds?

2) How will you foster an attitude of listening to the Word of God instead of to the wounds in your life?

Prayer About Listening to the Word, Not to the Wounds

All healing God, you invite me every day to read and listen to your holy Word; it's my daily bread. But so often in life I don't devote the time necessary to read or listen. Send your Spirit to me so that I can listen to your Word with the ears of my heart. May that same Holy Spirit help me unite my wounds to Christ's wounds, because it's by His wounds that we're healed. Amen.

Strategy 17: Understand and Use Your Imagination

"... you must change and become like little children. Otherwise, you will never enter the kingdom of heaven." —Matthew 18:3

The power of the imagination has been used for years to help people heal and succeed because the brain can be conditioned by our imagination. Whether that success is in sports, business, relationships, or healing stress, the imagination can help when used properly. God gave us the great gift of our imagination, and as Christians we need to understand its intrinsic power and use it to bring healing to our stressors and anxiety. *Don't use this recommendation if you have PTSD or other serious disorders. Seek out medical advice or counseling first.* If you want to continue with this idea, here's one way you can start to condition your brain through using your imagination:

Start by filling out the "Situation — Feelings Commitment" on the next page. If you have multiple situations in which you feel stressed, take one at a time and start with the one that you believe the Lord is calling you to conquer. There are more of these commitments in the "Cut-Out Reminders" section. I invite you to put the date on it so you can see your progress.

This commitment sheet will help you keep track of what feelings are going on during that stress, as well as how much anxiety or stress you feel in a specific situation on a scale of one through 10. The situation could be giving a presentation at work, being in a crowd, driving in traffic, seeing a dog or other animal, or any other situation that increases your stress when you encounter it.

Whatever the stress is, please take time to write down all the physical symptoms you feel when you're in the stressful situation. Be specific in the "what you are feeling" line because this will help you see your stress response diminish.

For example, if you write down that your heart rate increases, take your heart rate so you know what your typical heart rate is. An easy and quick way to do this is to place your pointer finger and your middle finger together over the pulse on the bottom of your wrist. Place these two fingers together on the center of the bottom of your wrist, press down gently and move slightly up or down and you should feel your pulse. (Never take your pulse with your thumb because there's a pulse in your thumb and you'll get an error.) Once you find your pulse, check it for six seconds, multiply by 10 and that's your beats per minute. There are other symptoms you want to note on the "what you are feeling" line as well, e.g., palms get sweaty, feel panicky, doubt, etc. The more specific you are, the better you can track your responses.

> **Situation — Feelings Commitment Using My Imagination**
>
> *Don't use this page if you have PTSD or other serious disorders. Seek out counseling.*
>
> When I encounter this_____
>
> _____
>
> _____
>
> (write down what you're doing or where you are when you're stressed)
>
> This is what I feel_____
>
> _____
>
> _____
>
> (write down your major feelings: doubt, fear, heart races—perhaps include beats per minute—panic, etc.)
>
> On a scale of 1 – 10 (10 = the highest) this is how stressed out I am in this situation: _____
>
> *I now commit to using my God-given gift of imagination for 10 to 15 minutes a day to lower my stressful response to this situation.*
>
> Signature_____Date_____

Now that you've completed the commitment, here's how you'll use your imagination to initiate some healing for this situation:

First, find a quiet room and begin with a short prayer asking the Holy Spirit to guide your imagination as you use it to literally create a new response to any stress. **Next, use all five senses** when possible (touch, sight, sound, hearing, smell, and taste) and imagine yourself encountering the situation that causes you stress.

For example, if you're stressed out about being in public, you'll want to: see the room you are in and the people around you, hear the sounds, feel the wall, taste the food if you're eating, etc. When you imagine the source of your anxiety, you might start to feel anxious, and when you feel anxious, imagine practicing one or more of your favorite recommendations in this workbook. Then start to feel your stress response lessen as you're able to relax more and more in the imagined situation. Try to imagine the stressful encounter several times, and each time imagine a more peaceful response with all five of your senses. This way, by the time you actually encounter the real (unimagined) stressor, your mind will have been there dozens or hundreds of times, with a lower stress response.

If your first number was "9," practice having an "8" response by using your favorite recommendations in this workbook. See yourself using these recommendations successfully and feel your stress response go down. While you're imagining an "8" response, pay close attention to your feelings that make up that "8" response and how it's slightly less stressful than the feelings you felt with a "9" response. For example, maybe with a "9" you wrote down that your heart rate was 100 beats a minute. When you imagine an "8" response, you might realize that your heart rate is lower.

After you've practiced every day using your imagination this way for about two weeks or so, or when you feel comfortable, I invite you to try to actually encounter the situation that causes your stress. You may want to bring a cross or a small Bible with you as a reminder that Jesus is with you, or go with a loved one. If, when you're actually physically encountering the stress and it becomes too much, simply leave, go home and use your imagination again. Maybe this time imagine yourself using many, or different, recommendations in this workbook.

When you actually encounter the stress, I invite you to write that response down as well and date it. Keep track of it and see the positive difference that imagination can make in your stress level. Feel that difference and write it down on your "Follow-Up Chart." You can find two of these follow-up charts in the "Cut-Out Reminders" section of this workbook so you can track your progress with multiple stressors and with multiple follow-ups. Put the date on them so you can see your progress. Feel free to copy these charts for your own use.

Prayer About Using My Imagination

Oh God, you have created me with the power of imagination. Help me learn to use this gift to practice new responses to stressful situations. Send your Holy Spirit so that I can be disciplined enough to practice these imagination techniques. May your love for me continue to encourage me as I create new, healthier responses to old sources of stress in my life. I ask this through Christ our Lord and in your Spirit's power. Amen.

Strategy 18: Examine the Difference Between Shame and Guilt

"Truth will continue forever, but lies are only for a moment."
—Proverbs 12:19

Too many of us believe that shame and guilt are the same realities, but I don't think they are. In fact, I think guilt is a great gift from God. Guilt is a built-in mechanism that tells us we've done something that we ought not to have done.

Shame is a wicked tool used by the evil one. I do find it striking that both shame and guilt quote Scripture. Have you ever noticed that? They both rightly remind us that "We are sinners." But it's only shame, in its cunning way, that conveniently leaves out the fact that "We have been redeemed!" Yes, shame wants us focusing only on our sin. Shame deeply desires that we forget all of the powerful ramifications of being redeemed in the Blood of the Lamb. Guilt, on the other hand, gets it right. Guilt tells us that "We are sinners, and we have been redeemed." Guilt continues, "Repent of the mistake you just made, ask God and others (if applicable) for forgiveness, forgive yourself and let God love you and bring good from your mistake." That's a striking contrast to the lies of shame.

What does this have to do with stress or anxiety? Everything! I remember working with Paula. She had never thought of the difference between shame and guilt and actually thought it is holy to carry around a little shame. After all, she's a sinner, as we all are. When we examined that notion we discovered that the shame she was carrying around was weighing her down quite noticeably. If we believe we are sinners (and don't think about how we are redeemed) then it's perfectly fine to beat ourselves up and create stress in our life so that things don't get "too good." After all, we're sinners. Shame is cunning and we need to recognize the lie of it. Once Paula understood the difference between guilt and shame, she could start deciding which one she wanted to listen to. When she felt shame, she started telling herself she didn't need to listen to the lie of shame anymore. This helped lower her stress and anxiety and she experienced more peace in her life. Such is the power of the love of God!

So the next time you hear shame and guilt used synonymously, perhaps invite others to think about how yes, they both quote Scripture, but only guilt gets it right.

Reflection Questions About the Difference Between Shame and Guilt

1) Have you found yourself believing that you need to beat yourself up a little bit? After all, you're a sinner, or so shame would say.

2) If you've fallen into the trap that shame lays out, what can you do today to become free from those snares?

Prayer About the Difference Between Shame and Guilt

Oh good and loving God, you have given me the gift of a conscience to tell me when I am not following your loving way. Help me always to inform my conscience well so that I can see clearly the difference between shame and guilt. Please send your Holy Spirit so that, after learning this valuable lesson myself, I may teach it to someone else in need. Amen.

Strategy 19: The Muscle of Music

"Blossoms appear through all the land. The time has come to sing; the cooing of doves is heard in our land." —Song of Songs 2:12

Music has an innate ability to help or hinder our stress levels. It has a muscle that can be used to sadden our mood (think about a melancholy melody), it can be used to agitate our mood (think about a more caustic melody, like heavy metal), and it can be used to lift our mood (think about a happy melody). One of my Christian accountability brothers (and co-therapist at the clinic) told me a story about the muscle of music that beautifully exemplifies this truth.

His wife was babysitting their one-year-old grandson and they were listening to a classical music radio station. The music was uplifting and energizing and they were dancing and singing and having a great time. The next selection was a piece written in a minor key and had a dirge-like quality. Immediately their little grandson's mood changed. He started to cry. He wasn't hungry, wet, or alone, but in his sad mood he was nearly inconsolable. He was grief stricken by the selection of music that his little brain was processing. After the piece was finished, his mood changed again, and he was dancing and singing. This powerfully true story clearly shows the impact of the muscle of music.

I know this is true in my life as well. When I'm feeling stressed out or agitated, good Christian music will frequently help to life my mood. I love that my cell phone has an MP3 player because it's full of Christian music I can listen to when I need a pick-me-up. Or I'll go to the Psalms when I'm stressed and find one I can sit with and let it lower my stress. (The Psalms were originally set to music and are very powerful.) I usually have Christian music on in the background while I'm washing the dishes for the third time before lunch, washing clothes, doing arts and crafts with the kids, or anything else I need to do for the day. Music has been a powerful antidote to stress in my life and I thank God for it. I invite you to think about how the muscle of music is being used in your life; does it help or hinder your stress levels?

Reflection Questions About the Muscle of Music

1) Have you noticed how music can help or hinder your stress levels? If not, how can you use music to lower your stress levels?

2) The Psalms were originally set to music and can be very soothing. Do you turn to the Psalms to find comfort in the midst of your stress? If not, try it and see how comforting they can be as they validate your feelings. If you find one that's less than comforting, perhaps skip over it for the time being. After doing this, take time to write down the peace they bring:

Prayer About the Muscle of Music

Oh God who sings over me, I thank you for the gift of music you give me every day. Help me to understand how powerful music is. Send me your Holy Spirit as I carefully choose the music I need in life to lower my stress. I ask this through Christ our Lord, and in the power of your Spirit. Amen.

Strategy 20: Lessons from Your Family of Origin and the Origin of Family

"God did this so He could buy freedom for those who were under the law and so we could become His children." —Galations 4:5

A workbook on stress wouldn't be complete without a discussion on the first place we learned how to deal or not deal with stress . . . our family of origin. The family that we were raised in taught us so much about stress and anxiety—whether right or wrong, good or bad, it taught you. Maybe your family taught you by not saying anything at all but by their actions. Maybe your family taught you to drink when you get stressed. Maybe your family taught you to pray or become angry when you get stressed. These are all responses I have heard from clients when I ask them this question: When's the last time you prayerfully examined your family of origin and what it taught you about stress management? Take a minute to think about that question. If this is too difficult, I recommend that you skip this and seek professional help to work through these hurts; remember that God has good plans for you and can bring healing from these past hurts. If you're able to, write down the major points that you learned from your family about dealing with stress, and start with the positives.

As you go through the lessons taught in your family of origin, especially the negative ones, remember that you're first a child of God and that the Holy Spirit can help to bring new life to all the difficulties that your family of origin may struggle with (more about that later in this chapter).

1) Positive ways my parent(s)/guardian taught me how to manage stress:

2) Negative ways my parent(s)/guardian taught me what to do with stress:

Now, take a look at that list. Are there any items you may need to grieve? If so, you can go to page 29 so you can grieve with hope. Are there any items you need to forgive? If so, go to page 25 and read about forgiveness fundamentals. If there are any negative lessons on your list, you can eventually try this with them: re-write them (then erase them from the list) and give them to God by safely burning them.

Many people love to privately write down all of their family of origin hurts and then safely burn the paper. If you choose to do this, watch the ritual. Watch the burning. The ash is a different substance from the paper (a chemical change). And ash can be used as a fertilizer! This is exactly what God wants to do with your hurts as well. Romans 8:28 promises us that the Holy Spirit will turn our hurts into good when we love God. But in order for that healing to happen we need to give our hurts over to God. If we hold on to our hurts too tightly, God respects our free will and may not transform them into the abundant life the Holy Spirit wants for us.

Yes, examining family of origin is important, but it's not more important than examining the origin of family (God). Remember who you are? You are a child of God. I hope by now you're telling yourself daily about your great identity. If you aren't, please go back to page 23 and review that chapter again.

I say that origin of family is more important than family of origin. Why? If we forget who we are, then the wounds from our family of origin will fight hard to give us a false "identity," and in our brokenness we sometimes believe this false "identity." (we discussed this on page 51). So we need to remind ourselves of our identity every day and truly believe that origin of family is more important than family of origin.

The truth about your origin of family is that God loves you. God has specific and good plans for you! God "waited" (so to speak) a long time for you, and now here you are on this earth, reading this workbook. God desires to bring healing from any stress and anxiety that you have felt. And not only that, but God can also bring good from all the pain you will ever go through. As you work through your family of origin and how it taught you (or didn't teach you) to deal with stress, may you continue to become more of who you already are: a precious and powerful child of the King.

Reflection Questions About Family of Origin and Origin of Family

1) What's a new insight you've received from this recommendation?

2) How will this new insight help you today to respond to stressors or anxiety?

3) Look again at your list of positive and negative lessons and today, work on changing just one of the negative things you have learned about stress management. Which one will that be, and how will you do it?

Prayer About Family of Origin and Origin of Family

Oh God, you have created my family; you are the origin of all family life. And yet, in our brokenness your love sometimes isn't communicated in our families as you desire. Please send me your Holy Spirit as I sort out ways that my family taught me to deal with stress. May the Spirit of new life continue to give me hope as I focus on my great identity as one of your children. Amen.

Strategy 21: The New is in the Now

"So, just as Christ was raised from the dead by the wonderful power of the Father, we also can live a new life." —Romans 6:4

Beth talked to me, feeling all stressed out: "Jim, if I could just get to April 24, then I will be less stressed." Yet that date was six weeks away! Maybe she didn't realize it, but Beth was putting her finger on a big stressor for many of us: by-passing the power of the present moment for the "promise" of a calmer tomorrow. I listened to her, validated her, and then started telling her about how "the new is in the now."

The Gospel of John has much to teach us about stress and anxiety. This deeply theological gospel was the last one written. Most scholars agree that it was written about 70 years after Jesus died. That means that the early Christians had several decades after Christ's death to reflect on what it means to be a Christian in this world.

The Gospel of John uses the phrase "eternal life" about 18 times, which is more than the other three Gospels put together. Moreover, many times when the term "eternal life" is used in John, it's preceded by a present tense verb! That means that in the Gospel of John the early Christians didn't make a distinction between the historical resurrection of Jesus (the day Jesus actually rose from the dead) and the eternal life that Christ's life, death, resurrection, and sending of the Spirit brings us today. This is a message that we need to shout from the rooftops!

That means that the resurrection is not only a historical fact, but it's a present reality because the resurrection encompasses all time. How often in our lives do we think about that? How often do we think that this moment, right now, is already infused with the power of the resurrection? This moment right now has already been redeemed and the Holy Spirit desires to bring new life to me now from all of my "death" experiences. In other words, the new is in the now.

This has tremendous implications for stress management, pain management, anger management, anxiety, depression, and anything else we humans can experience. The Holy Spirit has already redeemed our pain and wounds. Christ has already won the victory; all we need to do is say "Yes" and participate in that awesome gift every day. When Beth heard that, she loved it and it helped lower her stress. I had to learn this as well, and it changed my life.

I had no idea how God was going to use the pain of my being diagnosed with Generalized Anxiety Disorder (GAD) in 1996. I mean really, I was a therapist and I was supposed to know about this kind of thing. But slowly the Holy Spirit encouraged me to participate in Christ's resurrection by seeking out help, which I did from my spouse, my spiritual director, and other brothers from Church. So now, through the Holy Spirit's blessing, I can use that experience of being diagnosed with GAD to help others with stress and anxiety, and even use it to write a workbook so that others can find a way towards healing, as I did. This had nothing to do with me. This had everything to do with the resurrection anointing my pain and bringing forth new life from it, just as Christ wants to do in your life today.

Too many times we Christians think about the resurrection in just two ways. These ways aren't wrong; they're just not the full truth, because we limit God's almighty power:

1) Jesus historically rose from the dead.

2) We will rise from the dead as well when Christ comes in glory or when we die.

As I mentioned, these aren't wrong ways to think about the resurrection, but they're certainly incomplete. If we want to learn from the Gospel of John we need to add another way of thinking about the resurrection, which will have a direct impact on stress in our life:

3) Christ's resurrection was so powerful that it encompasses all of time (it's transtemporal) and brings new life to everyone redeemed in his love! Today!

My prayer is that this truth will guide all you do today. Maybe you're filled with anxiety, stress, or worry right now. If you are, I'm sorry. I know how it feels. Maybe take a minute right now, place your hand over your heart and say "I'm feeling worried (or stressed) right now, but I know Christ's new life can work through this and bring good from it eventually." That doesn't take away the pain, but it does offer a context of hope so you can understand what I now understand: the new is in the now, and God can and will bring good from this suffering you are going through. I learned it, Beth learned it, and I know you can, too.

Reflection Questions About The New is in the Now

1) What does it mean to you that you have the power of the resurrection in your life today?

2) What are some "death" areas in your life where God desires to bring about new life?

3) How is God calling you to participate in bringing about new life from the "deaths" you wrote about in question 2? (for example, God was calling me to seek out help, and I'm glad I did). What might God be calling you to?

Prayer About The New is in the Now

All good and comforting God, you know when I am hurting and in pain. And you desire to send people into my life to help carry that pain so that I can participate in Christ's all powerful resurrection. Please send your Holy Spirit to give me the courage and strength to take part in the great mystery and cycle of death, which always gives way to new life. Amen.

Strategy 22: Got Anger? Get a Plan

"When you are angry, do not sin . . ." —Ephesians 4:26

Robin came to me with a lot of anger. She was fuming, and she had a right to be. I validated her anger and then discussed with her what I'm about to share with you. She loved these ideas and has been using them for a while now. We journeyed together for about half a year, and at the end of our therapy, she smiled at me and said, "You know, I'm much less angry now, and I even lost weight!" That's the sign of a good anger plan.

Anger is a universal human feeling. Every human on earth has felt it, including Jesus our Lord. The Bible is full of the dangers of anger. Yet in Ephesians 4:26 there is a powerful invitation to "be angry and sin not," and in Psalm 76 we read that "Our anger will serve to praise you." These passages invite us to understand that the feeling of anger is not the problem. In fact, we need to feel our feelings of anger and process them in a healthy way; to do something positive with our anger so it doesn't do something negative with us. Sometimes anger is telling us that something isn't right in a relationship or that an injustice has been done. There are many reasons we feel angry.

When we're honest, we see that anger and stress can create and exacerbate each other. So what we need to do is get a plan. The first step in this plan is to understand what creates the feelings of anger inside of us. In other words, what are your anger "triggers?" By identifying these triggers we may be able to decrease our negative anger responses (yelling, road rage, not treating each other respectfully, etc.). Take a moment now to name your anger responses. . . what triggers the feelings of anger inside you?

It isn't always practical or realistic to say that all we have to do is avoid these triggers and life will be fine. So we need to have a second part to our plan: what to do when I can't avoid a trigger and I become angry? There are many ways to navigate this. One concept I teach is the "anger/stress safe."

The "safe" I'm referring to (for me) is a titanium-built, re-enforced safe that our Lord holds (for added security). Every time you feel stressed out or angry, learn to feel the feeling without acting on it right away. Then, open up the safe and make a secure deposit. Next, you need to empty the safe productively so it doesn't weigh you down—making you depressed or anxious—or explode—leading to outbursts that you don't want. These are two options that must be avoided. My "safe" is titanium-built; what does your "safe" look like?

There are three major keys to the idea of an "anger/stress safe." The first is recognizing who we are as children of God and how we have dominion over stress and anger in our lives. In other words, we can name our feelings and we don't have to be enslaved by them. Because we belong to Christ, we share in Christ's power to have dominion over these dynamics. If this is a new concept to you, spend some time thinking about it. Christ is the "Lord of Lords," and we share in Christ's identity, as 1st Peter and many other scripture verses inform us. Therefore, we share Christ's dominion as well, and we can use that dominion to help us with anger and stressful feelings. They don't own us; we own them.

The second key is to feel the feeling: don't suppress or deny anger or stress, and don't act on it right away, because this will only make it worse! Train yourself to say something like, "I am angry now" or "I am stressed out right now" or "I am hurt right now" and then put those feelings in your "anger/stress safe" and tell them "I will deal with you later." I call this the "contain and maintain" key of anger management. Feel the feelings, but "contain" them in your safe and then "maintain" what you were doing until you can productively empty the safe.

The third key is to productively empty the safe periodically—two to four times a week at least. You must devote time to do something positive with these feelings so they don't do something negative with you. These feelings are not bad, but what we do or don't do with them can be bad or good. The "anger/stress safe" is here to teach you how to eventually harness the feelings productively.

You can write out the contents of your emotional safe and then safely burn the paper. If you choose to do this, watch the ritual. The ash is a different substance from the paper: a chemical change. And ash can be used as a fertilizer! This is exactly what God wants to do with our stress and anger. Romans 8:28 promises us that God will turn our hurts into good when we love God. But in order for that healing to happen, we need to give our stress and anger to God. If we hold on to them too tightly, God respects our free will and may not transform them into the abundant life God wants for us.

Maybe you don't like to write but prefer to exercise out your anger or stress. If this is the case, you can start to do a workout, and when you start sweating, open up your anger/stress safe and use it as fuel. I've used this technique many times and I always feel like a new man after my workout. If you use this to empty your "safe," watch the symbolism. When we perspire we release physical toxins from our bodies. So when we think about emptying our "safe" while we sweat, we're releasing emotional feelings as well as physical toxins. It's a great symbol and one I use frequently.

Maybe you want to simply do some deep breathing where you prayerfully open your emotional safe, give the contents to God, and let God heal and resurrect the feelings. Or perhaps you may want to talk to a trusted individual about these emotions. Whatever the strategy, the more you use your emotional safe, the more you teach your stress and anger, and ultimately all your feelings, that you can harness them and you own them; they don't own you.

You can use any other image that works for you if the "anger/stress safe" doesn't work, but I invite you to try to come up with an image that works for you, because our imaginations are powerful and have been under-utilized in stress and anger management.

Personally, I love using the anger/stress safe in my life. When stress comes in or I'm angry at the driver in front of me for cutting me off, I address the anger and "put" it in my anger safe. I will say something like, "I am angry about that, and I am going to put you (my anger feelings) in my safe and I will deal with you later when I am able." Then I take a few deep breaths and pray and I'm on my way to a healthier day. At least two to three times a week I intentionally "empty" it via prayer, exercising, and communication. Those are my top three strategies to deal with stress and anger in my life. What about you?

Reflection Questions About Got Anger? Get a Plan

1) Do you like the concept of an "anger/stress safe?" If so, can you see using it today?

2) If you don't like the concept of a "safe," what other concept can you use?

3) Have you ever considered that you have dominion (or control) over your anger so you can use it and it doesn't have to use you? How does that concept help you with your anger today?

Prayer About Got Anger? Get a Plan

All powerful God, you understand anger, and through your son Jesus you have redeemed it and every feeling. May your Holy Spirit bless me so that I can see the power that you share with me. I do not have to be controlled by anger, stress, or any feeling through my life in Christ. Help me create and use a plan to harness my anger and stress. I pray this through Christ our Lord and in your Holy Spirit. Amen.

Strategy 23: G.I.G.O. Applies to Stress and Anxiety

"You should know that your body is a temple for the Holy Spirit who is in you." —I Corinthians 6:19

The Word so beautifully reminds us that we are good people and that we are temples of the Holy Spirit (I Cor. 6:19). We're invited by our loving God to take care of the bodies that God gave us. When we become better stewards of our temples, we see that stress and anxiety levels can lessen.

Do you remember the G.I.G.O. principle? It's an old computer acronym for "Garbage In, Garbage Out." This applies directly to stress and anxiety when we recognize the sources of "garbage" in our society that we sometimes consume. With the power of the Holy Spirit working through these recommendations, we can change this to "Good In, Good Out." When we do this changing work, we can have continual healing and a sense of calm in our lives.

In this section I highlight some areas I've seen as a therapist and coach that increase our stress as it relates to who we are as humans. Most Christians would agree with the idea that humans have at least three dimensions: body, mind, and soul. Ideally, there's an integration of these three areas in our life. But when we have high stress or anxiety, it can lead to a terrible disintegration. I address them separately only to point out how if one area is out of sync, it can have a ripple effect on the other two areas and can increase our stress and anxiety. I'm not prioritizing them, but I'll start with the body.

G.I.G.O. Areas for Your Body

• **Watch emotional eating and substance use** (caffeine, nicotine, etc.). Emotional eating is something I tried when I was wrestling with anxiety. Turning toward food is tempting because simple carbohydrates (chips, candy, pop, white bread, pasta, etc.) will make you feel better initially bio-chemically (with your brain chemistry). The problem is that too many of these simple carbohydrates can lead to being overweight, and that's a stress on our bodies. Caffeine and nicotine are stimulates so they increase our heart rate and can increase our stress levels.

Be aware of alcohol because it leaves the brain with a net deficit of serotonin, a brain chemical linked to good mood, and it does many other things as well. If you're going to drink, most professionals would agree that the "acceptable" amount of alcohol is one daily "standard drink" for a woman and two daily "standard drinks" for a man. There's a different acceptable amount based on sex because women metabolize alcohol differently than men. A "standard drink" is one five ounce glass of wine, one shot of whiskey, or one 12 ounce can of beer. You can't "save them up" and have seven drinks on a Friday night; that's not healthy. I also typically add that if you're drinking every day you may want to think about that habit in your life, even if it's only one drink for a woman and two drinks for a man.

• **Know and practice good sleep hygiene**. The bedroom should be used only for four purposes: prayer, getting dressed, sleeping, and marital intimacy. Stop consuming caffeine at least eight hours before you go to sleep. If you nap, keep it to a minimum. No TV in your bedroom and keep your bedroom as dark as possible. Have a nighttime ritual that includes a time to relax (see some of the relaxation ideas on page 40?). Possibly keep a dream journal by your bed for writing your dreams down when you wake up. If you prematurely wake up and can't get back to sleep within five or 10 minutes, remember that the bedroom is only for four purposes, so get out of bed (quietly if married), and read some comforting Psalms until you're tired enough to get back to sleep.

• **Consistently eat a good breakfast**, and choose low glycemic foods throughout the day so your sugar levels don't spike. Spiking blood sugar levels lead to drowsiness, which we usually mask with a shot of caffeine. You can do an Internet search to find some foods with low glycemic values.

• **Sip plenty of clean water** throughout the day, and eat more slowly.

- **Use a stress star or stress ball** throughout the day. They're made of a pliable material and it feels good to squeeze them hard when stress is high. Try some gentle stretches for your body; start slowly if you aren't used to this. You can purchase these online or at a craft store.

- **Make time to exercise**: cardio and strength training, three to four times a week. If this is a new practice for you, start slowly and with your doctor's approval.

- **Make sure you're sleeping at least seven to eight hours each night**. More and more sleep research is showing us that it doesn't pay to try to stay up later in order to be productive. The body needs sleep to regenerate itself.

Reflection Questions About G.I.G.O. for Your Body

1) Of the seven G.I.G.O. areas for your body, which one(s) speaks to you today?

2) When will you start to make those changes?

G.I.G.O. Areas for Your Mind

- **Take time to laugh daily!** When we laugh, our brain releases endorphins, morphine-like chemicals, which can make us feel really good. Try not to take yourself too seriously, but don't be sarcastic toward yourself or others. The root word for sarcastic is from the Greek meaning "flesh," and can be translated as "tearing off the flesh." Never use sarcasm as humor. When we do, we rip the flesh off that relationship. . . whether it's a relationship with others or ourselves.

Our family loves to pull out old home movies when the kids were younger. We think this is a good use of screentime, and it always makes us laugh. God has a wonderful sense of humor, so laugh with God, by yourself, and with others daily!

- **Monitor what you watch on TV, movies, and the Internet**. Most of our "entertainment" is not entertaining at all. It's offensive to God and the law of love, and because of that it increases our anxiety, even unconsciously. That's not a very popular notion, but it's true. We have no idea about the long-term consequences of the epidemic of watching too much stuff on TV, or any screen, for that matter. My invitation is for families to try to live without TV for a week and see what happens. Once you get away from it for a little bit, you quickly begin to see how relationships can grow through games, reading, talking, and walking. Also, when we're away from the TV for awhile, we see how toxic it truly is.

• **Watch what you read**. Many of the secular newspapers, magazines, and other print sources are toxic to our mind. We need to feed our minds good food. Reading good materials is one way to do that. Christian novels, Christian news sites, and Christian magazines can all be a better alternative to secular sources for staying informed.

• **Watch what you tell yourself**. This is so important that it has its own chapter (Strategy 25, page 81). If you find yourself with the nasty habit of telling yourself negative things, please go through the strategy "Name and Re-write Your Negative MP3 Files."

Reflection Questions About G.I.G.O. for Your Mind

1) Of the four G.I.G.O. areas for your mind, which one(s) speaks to you today?

2) When will you start to make those changes?

G.I.G.O. Areas for Your Soul

• **Let God love you**. Pray. Just sit today for three minutes and let God love you. So often we are so busy that we don't even stop to recognize that God is so in love with us and desires good things in our lives. Take time today to let God love you; it's a wonderful way to feed your soul.

• **Practice intentional silence**. There's so much noise in our world, and yet silence remains God's first language. Practice silence today and see how much it feeds your soul.

- **Read the Word of God**, daily if possible. I remember once when I talked about this topic, and the response was rather surprising. The person said, "We don't have time for that, not like the preacher." He may have been right that we don't have time to devote "like a preacher" does, because many preachers spend hours on one sermon. But I replied, "Really? How much time do you have to watch TV?" There was no further conversation. That's what has happened in some households. The TV is more important than the Word of God. We need to reverse this trend so we can connect to the source of life itself: the living Word of God.

- **Go on a retreat!** I love retreat time; in fact, some of this workbook was written while on retreat and I was praying for you! A retreat can be a half-day of quiet or it can be overnight. Ease into it if you've never been on one. In central Minnesota we are blessed to have several retreat centers. Ask your pastor or a friend for more information and suggestions. I firmly believe we can't advance unless we retreat.

- **Practice** *Lectio Divina* (Latin for "Holy Reading"). This is a wonderful ancient Christian practise. Basically, it involves reading a passage of Scripture slowly and meditatively and then allowing the Holy Spirit to speak to our lives through that passage. Then, read it again slowly and intentionally and see if there's a word or a phrase that impresses you in a particular way. Sit with that word or phrase and see what the Lord desires to tell you regarding that word or phrase. It's a time-honored way to feed your soul.

- **Appreciate beauty**. God created beauty, and when we go to a symphony to hear beauty or to an art gallery to see beauty, or to a library and check out a book with beautiful art, we glorify God and feed our soul. I love seeing beauty outside! Watching the moon, the stars, going hiking, canoeing, or swimming are all about appreciating natural beauty. With the Internet we don't even have to leave our houses to see and appreciate fine art, but there's nothing like seeing it in person.

- **Go to Church on Sunday**. With some, this isn't a very popular notion, but it's in the Ten Commandments: "Keep holy the Lord's day." I delight when someone tells me, "I connect with God in the woods, so I don't go to church." I think that's great; I love the woods as well. Yet that isn't the point of going to church on Sunday (or on Saturday, when some churches also offer services). The point of going to church on a weekly basis is that God knows we need community and God has asked us to worship weekly. It's a great way to feed your soul.

- **Analyze, know, and be vigilant about your primary sources of temptation.** I've been doing licensed therapy since 1996, and in my humble opinion many males sin with their eyes (lust) and many females sin with their ears and mouth (gossip). Obviously, there are other areas that we all wrestle with as well. It's good to pray about and think about who we are as children of God so we develop habits that will help us avoid temptation. By knowing our primary sources of temptation we can become more of who we are as God's children. If you have a tendency to talk too much, perhaps pray daily with Psalm 141: "Set, O Lord, a guard over my mouth; keep watch at the door of my lips." What a wonderful prayer. The ancients had a hard time with talking too much, too. This prayer helped them, and it can help you.

If you have a hard time with lust, it might help to place the temptation in the truth. When you see someone you're attracted to, immediately say a prayer for that person and yourself. Tell yourself, "That person is a child of God and so am I." By doing this you will take what once was a temptation and turn it into a blessing.

Reflection Questions About G.I.G.O. for Your Soul

1) Of the eight G.I.G.O. areas for your soul, which one(s) speaks to you today?

2) When will you start to make those changes?

Prayer About Good In, Good Out for Body, Mind, and Soul

All loving God, you so tenderly provide for my needs of body, mind, and soul. Please send me your Holy Spirit so that I can continue to create opportunities to bring healing and balance in my life. May your love and care empower me to choose wisely how I tend to my body, mind, and soul so that they may ultimately glorify your name. I pray this through Christ our Lord in the power of your Holy Spirit. Amen.

Strategy 24: Use Productive and Proactive Recreation Time

"Then Jesus said to the Pharisees, 'The Sabbath day was made to help people; they were not made to be ruled by the Sabbath day.'" —Mark 2:27

I recall working with Tom. His children had gone to college and he and his wife were empty nesters. I had been inviting him to take up some productive hobbies to lower his stress. Finally, he came in and told me that his doctor diagnosed him with high blood pressure. I think that's what helped him decide to actually do some hobbies and not just talk about it with a therapist. When I saw him last he told me he was less stressed because he was playing golf every evening. His wife was happy about that and it helped him lower his stress. In fact, he also told me that his blood pressure was better. He immediately saw some healing when he devoted time to a productive hobby. We all need to do the same.

As humans we were created to have recreation in our lives. These hobbies that help us relax and become more of who we are as children of God are essential in stress management. When you think about the word recreation, it's literally "re" – "creation." That means that, ideally, our hobbies or recreational activities need to bring forth new creation within us. Because of this, God desires that we select hobbies that are productive in our lives instead of nonproductive pursuits.

Non-productive "hobbies" could be watching every football game for six hours on a Sunday, or shopping for hours and hours for things we really don't need. These are non-productive because they don't re-create us. Don't get me wrong—I like to watch a game of football too, but I try to exercise to it so that there's an element of re-creation activity in it. I also typically mute the commercials because they don't help me become more of who I am as a son of God.

If screentime or shopping isn't recreational, then what is? We need silence, meditation, appreciating beauty, art, music, prayer, conversation (especially with our loved ones), nature, journaling, exercising, gardening, sewing, teaching, reading, writing, singing, etc. All of these activities are very much re-creational and can eventually replace unproductive screentime and lower stress.

I also think our recreational times need to be proactive. Ideally, we need to actively participate in hobbies several times a week. When we don't make time for our hobbies we can start to feel like our wheels are just spinning and smoking but we're not going anywhere. Life can feel like a bunch of problems to be hashed out and waded through. When we have proactive hobbies it makes our lives healthier and happier. If you haven't made time for these, please don't put them off any longer. Open up your heart to their power and allow the Holy Spirit to re-create you through them.

Reflection Questions About Productive and Proactive Recreation Time

1) What are your favorite hobbies?

2) Have you devoted enough time to these hobbies?

Prayer About Productive and Proactive Recreation Time

All good and faithful God, you call me to open up my mind every day to activities that will help lower my stress and worry. These hobbies you give me are holy. Help me to recognize that, and to devote enough time to them. I pray this through Christ our Lord, and in the power of the Holy Spirit. Amen.

Strategy 25: Name and Re-Write Your Negative "MP3" Files

"Keep me from lying and being dishonest." —Proverbs 30:8

I enjoy facilitating workshops for various groups, and years ago I was giving a half-day workshop for a group of ministers. I started talking about the "tapes" we have in our lives and how they can impact our life negatively. During a break, one of the ministers came over and said, "You know those tapes you were talking about . . . I've got some of those!" I affirmed him by saying, "Yes, we all do" and we had a great talk about what to do with the negative "tapes" in our lives.

Years ago I called them tapes. Today I call them "MP3 files," because I want to stay current. My wife, Maureen, still likes to call them "tapes" but that's OK with me. So if "tapes" work better for you—or even 8-track tapes—that's great. No matter the name, they work the same. We all talk to ourselves; the question I ask is, "How Christian is my self-talk?" If it's negative, we have to change that now, because Christ demands that we love our neighbor as we love ourselves.

Negative MP3 files or tapes are lies that we believe about ourselves and tell ourselves sometimes consciously, sometimes unconsciously. I like the image of a cassette tape or MP3 file because both of these can be "re-recorded" into more positive self-talk. When our self-talk is mostly negative I can almost guarantee higher stress or anxiety. When we take time to "record" over them by the power of the Holy Spirit, and change them into more of a positive self-message, I can almost guarantee that we'll have less stress in our lives. This can be a challenge depending on our family of origin and other factors. Although it may be difficult to change these, through Christ's love and power it *is* possible.

We need to start the process of changing our negative self-talk into positive by first identifying a baseline of both negative and positive self statements. When I say positive self statements I don't mean egotistic or narcissistic statements. Nor do I mean accidentals such as those about hair color, eye color, being a good dresser, etc. Positive self-statements are made when I tell myself the truth about who I am as a child of God. For example, "I am a precious and powerful child of the King" is one of my favorites. These are the types of positive self-statements that I am referencing.

Take time to pray about this question, ask a trusted loved one, and be honest about this negative and positive self-talk baseline. When you have thought about it and prayed about it, please finish the reflection questions below.

Now work daily on lowering the negative number by at least one per day. If you need to, wear a rubber band on your wrist and gently "snap" yourself back into the truth when you catch yourself saying something negative to yourself. No welts, just a gentle reminder to not verbally beat yourself up. If you don't like that idea, then use the following idea.

If you're alone and you beat yourself up verbally, gently place your hand on your heart and tell yourself out loud, "I don't need to do that anymore; I can treat myself like a friend and be gentle with myself right now." Or use any other words that will help you avoid this behavior. None of us were born beating ourselves up emotionally or verbally; it's a learned behavior.

Reflection Questions About Creating Negative and Positive Self-talk Baselines

1) Write down the number of negative self-statements you tell yourself per day or per week:

2) Now write down the number of positive self-statements you tell yourself per day or per week:

3) Which number is greater?

If the positives are greater and you have zero negative self-statements, you're doing very well and probably can move beyond this recommendation. If, however, your negative numbers are greater than your positive numbers, or if you have no positive self-statements, continue to work on this behavior, because it can lower your stress and anxiety levels.

The good news is that with consistent and correct applications of these techniques we can learn not to do this destructive behavior and we can replace it with the truth of who we are as children of God.

Once you start learning how to stop the negative, then it's time to start the daily positive self-messages. It takes about 30 days for a new habit to take hold, so be gentle with yourself as you learn this.

Keep track of your victories in a "victory journal" so you can see how your new behavior is helping change the way you view yourself. The fewer negative MP3 files or "tapes" you have, the lower your stress can be.

Prayer About My "MP3 Files"

All knowing God, you understand me and you know when I talk negatively or positively about myself. Because I am your child, you want me to talk positively to myself, not negatively. Yet sometimes that is hard to do. Please send me your Holy Spirit to guide my self-talk so that I can talk to myself as I would to a best friend. I pray this through Christ our Lord, and in the power of the Holy Spirit. Amen.

Closing Thoughts

My hope and prayer is that these 25 strategies have created a more peaceful response to stress and anxiety in your life. I thank you for allowing me the privilege of sharing these ideas with you. I also hope that you have found the top seven or so strategies that work really well for you as you continue to develop healthier and holier responses to stress.

Again, I thank you for your attentiveness to these recommendations. May God bless you with a new day in Christ! Peace.

—Jim Otremba

Cut-Out Reminders

The following pages have some little reminders that I have taught over the years. For those of you who are open to learning new responses to stress and anxiety, these little statements can be powerful. I use these myself. I actually have one of them up on my bathroom mirror, and I sometimes put them in my smart phone. I know they work, even though at first glance it may seem a little peculiar, and even cheesy. I understand that. But I'm willing to risk being cheesy if helps at least one person develop newer, healthier responses to stress.

If you're going to use these reminders, I recommend that before you cut them out, take some packing tape and do a "daddy lamination." I've been using that technique for years with arts and crafts as a part-time stay-at-home dad. Put packing tape over both sides of the reminder you want, and then cut it out. The packing tape will act as an inexpensive way to laminate the card and will make it last for years.

New Stress Formula

When I'm stressed, I will associate it with prayer, an affirming word to myself, and deep breathing.

STRESS = Prayer, Affirming Word, Deep Breath

New Stress Formula

When I'm stressed, I will associate it with prayer, an affirming word to myself, and deep breathing.

STRESS = Prayer, Affirming Word, Deep Breath

This page left intentionally blank

Cut-Out Reminders

Here's the reminder we have on our bathroom mirrors:

I am a
child of *God.*
Treat me
accordingly.

I am a
child of *God.*
Treat me
accordingly.

This page left intentionally blank

Scriptural Truths About Who I Am

Read these every day. Choose at least three to memorize. When you start to tell yourself any negative messages, stop it with a rubber band around your wrist and a gentle snap (no welts, just a gentle snap back into the truth). If you don't like that idea, stop the negative self-talk by telling yourself "I don't need to tell myself that anymore." Then start telling yourself at least three of these truths instead every day. If none of these is helpful, feel free to do your own Bible search for different phrases to help you discover how much God loves you.

+ "We are God's children" (Romans 8:16).

+ "The Father has loved us so much that we are called children of God. And we really are his children" (I John 3:1).

+ "Don't be afraid, because I have saved you. I have called you by name, and you are mine" (Isaiah 43:1).

+ "No one will be able to defeat you all your life. Just as I was with Moses, so I will be with you. I will not leave you or forget you" (Joshua 1:5).

+ "Like babies you will be nursed and held in my arms and bounced on my knees. I will comfort you as a mother comforts her child" (Isaiah 66:12-13).

+ "I leave you peace; my peace I give you . . . So don't let your hearts be troubled or afraid" (John 14:27).

Scriptures quoted from *The Holy Bible, New Century Version®*, copyright © 1987, 1988, 1991 by Word Publishing, a division of Thomas Nelson, Inc. Used by permission.

Cut-Out Reminders

Situation - Feelings Commitment Using My Imagination

Don't use this page if you have PTSD or other serious disorders. Seek out counseling.

When I encounter this_____
(write down what you're doing or where you are when you're stressed)

This is what I feel_____
(write down your major feelings: doubt, fear, heart races—maybe include beats per minute—panic, etc.)

On a scale of 1 - 10 (10 = the highest) here's how stressed out I am in this situation: _____

I now commit to using my God-given gift of imagination for 10 to 15 minutes a day to lower my stressful response to this situation.

Signature_____Date_____

Situation - Feelings Commitment Using My Imagination

Don't use this page if you have PTSD or other serious disorders. Seek out counseling.

When I encounter this_____
(write down what you're doing or where you are when you're stressed)

This is what I feel_____
(write down your major feelings: doubt, fear, heart races—maybe include beats per minute—panic, etc.)

On a scale of 1 - 10 (10 = the highest) here's how stressed out I am in this situation: _____

I now commit to using my God-given gift of imagination for 10 to 15 minutes a day to lower my stressful response to this situation.

Signature_____Date_____

This page left intentionally blank

Follow-Up Chart

Follow-Up Chart

(Use after you actually encounter the stress you have been imagining)

Date_____

Today, after doing my imagination work, I actually encountered this stress:
_____

This is what I felt when I encountered this stress:
_____

(write down your major feelings: doubt, fear, heart races—maybe include beats per minute—panic, etc.) This reaction was (check one):

___ less stressful ___ about the same ___ more stressful than before my imagination work.

If your reaction was less stressful, the imagining you are doing is working well. Continue your great work! If your reaction was about the same or more stressful, you might want to do more imagination work with more (or different) strategies to lower your stress.

Follow-Up Chart

(Use after you actually encounter the stress you have been imagining)

Date_____

Today, after doing my imagination work, I actually encountered this stress:
_____

This is what I felt when I encountered this stress:
_____

(write down your major feelings: doubt, fear, heart races—maybe include beats per minute—panic, etc.) This reaction was (check one):

___ less stressful ___ about the same ___ more stressful than before my imagination work.

If your reaction was less stressful, the imagining you are doing is working well. Continue your great work! If your reaction was about the same or more stressful, you might want to do more imagination work with more (or different) strategies to lower your stress.

This page left intentionally blank

Post-Stress Snapshot Questionnaire

Take this only after you have practiced these recommendations 20 minutes a day for at least 30 days. Then compare your scores with your first Stress Snapshot Questionnaire. If the post score is not as low as you want it to be, continue practicing your favorites for 20 minutes a day and let the Lord bring healing. It may take a few months for your stress and anxiety to lower. It may have taken many months for your stress and anxiety to develop, so be patient as it heals. Don't lose heart; it took me many months to get into these habits of peace.

Date:_____

Circle the appropriate number for each item.
0 = Never 1 = Not Often 2 = Occasionally 3 = Frequently 4 = Mostly 5 = Always

When you're done, add up your total. There are three categories to this inventory: Body, Mind, and Soul/Relationships. I use three categories because stress and anxiety can alter different aspects of our lives. If you have severe symptoms of anxiety, please see your doctor as soon as possible.

Body

	Never	Not Oft.	Occasion.	Frequent.	Mostly	Always
1. Jaw tightness/clenching teeth	0	1	2	3	4	5
2. Heart racing	0	1	2	3	4	5
3. Stomach upset or "gurgling"	0	1	2	3	4	5
4. Headaches or migraines	0	1	2	3	4	5
5. Nervous habits (nail biting, etc.)	0	1	2	3	4	5
6. Muscle tightness	0	1	2	3	4	5
7. Back pain	0	1	2	3	4	5
8. Furrowed brow	0	1	2	3	4	5
9. Dizziness and/or chest pain	0	1	2	3	4	5
10. Unhealthy or emotional eating	0	1	2	3	4	5
11. Alcohol or drug misuse	0	1	2	3	4	5

Total from Body category = _____

(if there are serious Body stressors, please see your doctor immediately).

Mind

	Never	Not Oft.	Occasion.	Frequent.	Mostly	Always
12. Worry about things I can't change	0	1	2	3	4	5
13. Daily negative self-statements	0	1	2	3	4	5
14. Making mountains out of molehills	0	1	2	3	4	5
15. More pessimistic, less optimistic	0	1	2	3	4	5
16. Not sleeping well	0	1	2	3	4	5
17. Watching the nightly news	0	1	2	3	4	5
18. Feeling irrational fears	0	1	2	3	4	5
19. "Hamster on the wheel" thoughts	0	1	2	3	4	5
20. Perfectionist or "type A"	0	1	2	3	4	5
21. Reading negative articles or news	0	1	2	3	4	5
22. Watching secular movies	0	1	2	3	4	5
23. Watching secular TV	0	1	2	3	4	5

Total from Mind category = _____

Soul/Relationships

	Never	Not Oft.	Occasion.	Frequent.	Mostly	Always
24. Not being patient with self or others	0	1	2	3	4	5
25. Using harsh words	0	1	2	3	4	5
26. Using sarcasm or unhealthy tones	0	1	2	3	4	5
27. Not forgiving of others	0	1	2	3	4	5
28. Not forgiving of self	0	1	2	3	4	5
29. No regular public worship	0	1	2	3	4	5
30. Hopeless or helpless feelings	0	1	2	3	4	5
31. Lack of daily gratitude	0	1	2	3	4	5
32. Not much emotional or verbal closeness with others	0	1	2	3	4	5
33. Not many close friends I trust	0	1	2	3	4	5
34. My relationships feel hurtful	0	1	2	3	4	5
35. I don't feel respected by those who are supposed to love me	0	1	2	3	4	5
36. Negative image of God (God is only a judge and is harsh on you)	0	1	2	3	4	5

Total from Soul/Relationships category.............._____
Total from Body category (from page 94)........._____
Total from Mind category (from page 95)........._____

Grand Total..._____

Key

0 – 15...........Negligible Stress   16 – 30.........Low Stress
31 – 45.........Mild Stress   46 – 55.........Moderate Stress
56 – 80.........High Stress
81 – 180.......Severe Stress *(professional help is recommended)*

Notice: This questionnaire is not intended to be used for professional diagnostic purposes, nor is it a psychological inventory. The author assumes no liability for misuse of this questionnaire.
© 2009, James C. Otremba, M.Div., M.S., LICSW.

About the Author

Jim Otremba has been married to his best friend and soulmate, Maureen, since 1995. They have both been stay-at-home parents (part-time) since 1999.

Since 1996, Jim has worked with children, adults, families, and couples. He is the owner of the Center for Family Counseling, Inc., in St. Cloud, Minnesota, where he provides Christian counseling. (Visit **www.healinginchrist.com** for more information).

Jim holds a Master of Divinity degree from St. John's University (Collegeville, MN) and a Master's in Applied Psychology from St. Cloud State University. He is a Licensed Independent Clinical Social Worker in Minnesota and provides Christian life-coaching through **www.coachinginchrist.com**.

Jim and Maureen love to present workshops. If your church or congregation needs energetic, dynamic speakers, contact the Otrembas by email: jimotremba@gmail.com or maureenotremba@gmail.com.

They would be honored to work with your needs.

May God bless you and your family.

What Others Have Said About the Otrembas' Material

"I love learning concrete ways to deal with stress and anxiety."

"I really enjoyed the 'Daily Dozen' of stress—a much needed topic. Very practical advice and easy to apply."

"Thank you for your ministry—I'll be watching for your book and waiting for additional seminars."

"I thought it was really good and practical information that a person could take and use."

"The effective merging of physiology and Christianity... For effective and applied Christian living this was very good."

"... most practical and helpful in making immediate improvements within our marriage."

"We have been through many retreats and couples weekends—the spirituality of today's program was exceptional."   —*Married 44 years*

"Foundational Intimacies—It shined a light into an area of darkness, confusion, and isolation... It opened the door to dialoging without sniping and accusations. Our marriage was ROCKY, I saw little hope but now I feel hopeful. I can imagine possibilities, for the first time in many years."
—*Married 39 years*

"Helped to have time to talk about the things we struggle within our marriage and it offered ways, with Christ as the foundation, to help."
 —*Married 24 years*

"Foundational intimacies... we have been married 36 years and sometimes it feels like we are just roommates. I think the Foundational intimacies and a renewed focus on them could really help us improve our relationship. Thank you! Both of you (are) inspiring speakers, you can tell you live your faith well."

"It was helpful having experts in counseling and theology both! Often times we've experienced experts in one or the other. Having both together was extremely helpful. Excellent integration of counseling and theology."

"We'll be processing information for a long time, maybe the rest of our life. . . .very good; would recommend"   —*Married 18 years*

"Every couple came away with an enriched understanding of the spiritual aspect of our married life."

"We really enjoyed the passion and enthusiasm of your presentation. You both are very versed on the subject matter and your commitment to each other and to your faith was uplifting."

"Foundational intimacies . . . has been something I've been thinking about and wanting to talk about with my spouse for years, and now finally have."

"It was well worth our time to participate. I'm sure it has opened up discussion and actions for us that will be very helpful to us in continuing to grow our relationship."

"The talks on forgiveness were enlightening. I had not yet forgiven myself for a slight to my wife—although she had forgiven me . . ."

"I like the therapy perspective—it is nice to know that problems in marriage can be resolved and not just eat away or split up the marriage."

This page left intentionally blank

Made in the USA
Middletown, DE
15 April 2019